School Counselors and Censorship: Facing the Challenge

By

Greg Brigman and Peggy Moore

Library of Congress Cataloging-in-Publication Data

Brigman, Greg. 1951-

School counselors and censorship: facing the challenge / by Greg Brigman and Peggy Moore.

p. cm.

Includes bibliographical references.

ISBN 1-55620-140-0 : $24.95

1. Educational counseling—United States—Evaluation. 2. Developmental psychology. 3. Public schools—Censorship—United States. I. Moore, Peggy, 1942-   . II. American School Counselor Association. III. Title.

LB1027.5.B725 1994

371.4—dc20

94-14215
CIP

10 9 8 7 6 5 4 3 2 1

Printed in the United States of America.

American School Counselor Association

5999 Stevenson Avenue • Alexandria, Virginia 22304
703/823-9800 x388 • FAX: 703/461-3569

Editorial assistance and graphic design by
Educational Media Corporation®, Minneapolis, MN

About the Authors

Greg Brigman is a counselor educator at Clemson University where he coordinates the elementary and middle school counselor education programs. He was a middle school counselor from 1980 to 1990 and was the 1986 ASCA Middle School Co-Counselor of the Year. Dr. Brigman has worked in and with school systems experiencing challenges to counseling materials during the last 12 years. He has spent considerable time researching the censorship movement and the research base for effective counseling programs.

Peggy Moore is the Coordinator of Elementary Counseling Services in Oconee County, South Carolina. She spent nine months coordinating a model defense against a highly organized and intense effort to remove a counseling program (*PUMSY In Pursuit of Excellence*) in Oconee County. Ms. Moore has consulted with other counselor coordinators around the country, helping them through similar challenges. She is widely recognized in South Carolina as both a leader in promoting comprehensive developmental counseling and as an authority on managing challenges to counseling programs.

Acknowledgments

We wish to thank the many people and organizations who have contributed in the creation of this book:

- **The Elementary School Counselors of Oconee County** for their commitment to what is best for children.

- **The Administration and the counseling faculty at Clemson University** for their support and encouragement.

- **Denise McCormick,** a graduate assistant in the elementary counseling program at Clemson, for her organizational and research support.

- **Jennifer Adams,** a journalist, for her computer expertise, patience, and perseverance.

Greg Brigman and Peggy Moore

Table of Contents

- About the Authors iii
- Acknowledgments iv

Chapter 1

Introduction and Overview 1

What's Under Fire? 5

Main Issues Related to Challenges of School
Counseling Programs 6

Overview of Court, D.O.E., and School Board Decisions 7

Organizations that Support Developmental
School Counseling 15

Top Ten Suggestions for Managing a Challenge 16

Chapter 2

Research Support for Developmental Counseling 19

Developmental Counseling 22

Self-Esteem 24

Affective Education 25

Relaxation and Imagery 27

Thinking Skills and Cooperative Learning 27

PUMSY, DUSO, and Quest 28

Guidelines from U.S. Department of Labor and
National Education Organizations 44

Chapter 3

What to Expect from the Challengers 49

Far Right Organizations and Activists 51

Organizations Behind Most Challenges 52

Educational Agenda of the Far Right 54

Tactics and Techniques Used by the Far Right 56

"Hot-Button" Terms and the Language of Censorship 59

Arguments from the Censors 60

The Typical Censorship Scenario 61

Unless Effective Action is Taken 62

Chapter 4

An Ounce of Prevention: What to Do Before a
Challenge Occurs 63

ASCA Guidelines for Preventing Challenges 66

Proactive Strategies to Build Support for School
Counseling and Protect Students' Access to School
Counseling Programs and Materials 69

Summary of What to Do Before a Challenge Occurs 73

Chapter 5

A Pound of Cure: What to Do During a Challenge 75

ASCA Guidelines for Dealing with a Challenge 78

National School Board Guidelines for
Dealing With a Challenge 79

Strategies for Dealing with Tactics of Censorship Groups 86

Stretching the Hatch Amendment 91

Responses to Twelve Typical Concerns of Challengers 96

Chapter 6

Developing and Utilizing Community Support 101

Three Tools for Gaining Support 106

Letter Writing 107

Information Packets for Key Community Groups 116

Presentation to School Board and/or
Curriculum Review Committee 117

Involving the Media 123

Parent Networks 128

Other Key Groups to Contact for Support 139

Chapter 7

Helpful Organizations and Resources
When a Challenge Occurs 141

Organizations 143

Resources 145

Staying Up-To-Date 148

Chapter 8

Fundamentalism and the Schools 149

Key Points 151

Introduction: A Fundamentalist Complaint 152
Fundamentalism and Modernism 153

An Epistemological Debate 156
History Lessons 158

Fundamentalism and the Schools 161

Implications For Educators 165

A Final Note: Turning the Table 166

Appendices

Appendix A

**Sample Policy on Selection of
School Counseling Materials** 171

Appendix B

Sample Curriculum Review, Policy 172

Request for Reconsideration of Educational Materials ... 175

Appendix C

Sample Legal Opinion 176

Bibliography 177

"Since freedom of mind and freedom of expression are the roots of all freedom, to deny freedom in education is a crime against democracy."

John Dewey

Greg Brigman and Peggy Moore

Chapter 1

Introduction and Overview

- What's Under Fire?
- Main Issues Related to Challenges of School Counseling Programs
- Overview of Court, D.O.E., and School Board Decisions
- Organizations that Support Developmental School Counseling
- Top Ten Suggestions for Managing a Challenge

Greg Brigman and Peggy Moore

Chapter 1

Introduction and Overview

Censorship is on the rise and threatens the progress made in expanding developmental counseling programs. School counselors need to be proactive in order to ensure that children continue to receive the important skills training and information which form the core of a comprehensive developmental guidance program.

Developmental counseling is defined by Myrick as being based on developmental stages and tasks of children. The goal is to provide each student with the skills and experiences needed for school success and healthy development. Developmental counseling includes objectives related to (1) understanding self and others, (2) decision making and problem solving, (3) interpersonal and communication skills, (4) school success skills, and (5) career awareness skills (Myrick, 1993). These same areas are the frequent target of curriculum challenges.

Censorship, as related to school counseling, is defined by the American School Counselor Association's position statement on censorship as "the denial of a student's basic rights to receive any of the commonly recognized guidance and counseling services offered by school counselors." Two hundred sixty-four incidents of attempted censorship were reported in the United States in People For the American Way's (PFAW) *Attacks on the Freedom to Learn 1990-1991 Report*. The 1991-1992 total was a ten-year record of 376 challenges. While these two totals represent all curricular and library materials, counseling or counseling-related materials represented four of the five most frequently challenged materials in 1991-1992, and three of the ten most frequently challenged materials from 1982-1992. The top five for 1991-1992 were *PUMSY In Pursuit of Excellence*, *Impressions* (a reading series), *Quest*, *Positive Action*, and *DUSO (Developing Understanding of Self and Others)*. PFAW reported the success rate for challengers of all 1991-1992 challenges was 41 percent. Peterson and Poppen (1992b, p. 6) reported ways that 82 challenges to developmental guidance materials/programs had been resolved between 1988 and 1991. Sixteen of the 82 challenges (20%) were resolved by the school board or school officials halting or delaying the use of the materials/programs. Sixty six of the 82 challenges (80%) were resolved by school board or school officials ordering the continuation of the use of the materials/programs. (Six of the 66 required modifications before continuing use and 13 of the 66 permitted parents to withdraw their children from all or part of the program or required parental permission.)

This chapter focuses on clarifying the types of developmental counseling programs that are being challenged, the main issues involved in these challenges, an overview of pertinent court, D.O.E., and school board decisions, and organizations that support developmental counseling. Chapter 2 provides research support and national guidelines for developmental counseling. Chapter 3 looks at the organizations and activists behind most challenges, their strategies, and educational agenda. In Chapter 4, proactive measures aimed at preventing and/or preparing for future challenges are discussed. Chapter 5 deals with what to do when a challenge to counseling materials occurs. In Chapter 6, ideas for developing community support, including working with the news media, are presented. Chapter 7 highlights key organizations and resources that can help when a challenge occurs.

In Chapter 8, understanding the censorship movement from a historical and legal perspective is explored. To conclude, there are three appendices. The topics covered in the appendices are: • Appendix A: Sample Policy on Selection of School Counseling Materials • Appendix B: Sample Curriculum Review, Policy and Sample Forum for Request for Reconsideration • Appendix C: Sample Legal Opinion Regarding *PUMSY* and related programs.

What's Under Fire?

The following types of counseling or counseling-related programs have been most frequently challenged:

- **Developmental counseling**—Especially the preventive, classroom guidance component, which includes most, if not all, of the categories below.

- **Self-esteem programs**—Most prevention programs such as *Quest* and *Project Charlie*, as well as the programs listed below under Affective Education, include a self-esteem component. All developmental counseling programs include a self-esteem focus.

- **Affective education**—This is a broad category which includes social-emotional development programs such as *DUSO, PUMSY, Positive Action,* and *TAD*.

- **Relaxation and imagery**—These two are frequently cited as the most objectionable parts of the programs challenged.

- **Thinking skills and cooperative learning**—Programs which teach children to think critically, make decisions, solve problems, and which involve small group discussion are seen by some as undermining parental authority.

These programs, in addition to including school counselors, also involve regular classroom teachers in subjects such as social studies, language arts, health, home economics, gifted, and special education.

Because of the wide ranging impact to not only counselors and teachers but most importantly to children, it is essential for counselors to be aware of: (1) the main issues surrounding censorship challenges, (2) the findings of court cases, D.O.E., and school board rulings related to these challenges, and (3) educational research supporting challenged programs (Chapter 2). In addition to the above three, it is also very helpful for school counselors to know: (1) organizations supporting developmental counseling (Chapter 1), (2) organizations that offer assistance regarding censorship (Chapter 7), and (3) guidelines for handling a challenge to counseling programs (Chapters 4 and 5). To begin, the issues related to challenges of counseling materials and programs need to be clarified.

What are the Main Issues Related to Challenges of School Counseling Programs?

The four issues that seem to occur most frequently in challenges to counseling programs are:

- **Is the program advancing a particular religious philosophy and therefore violating the Establishment Clause of the U.S. Constitution?** Most frequently the claim is made that the program involves "New Age" practices such as hypnosis, meditation, guided imagery, Far Eastern religious concepts, or secular humanism.

- **Is the program violating the Hatch Amendment? More specifically, does the program constitute unauthorized psychological treatment and/or is it experimental?** The charge of "untrained" teachers or counselors conducting "therapy" in the classroom is usually part of this claim.

- **Is the program anti-family?** Rather than a legal issue, like the previous two issues, this charge is political in that it seeks to gain support of policy makers by portraying the challenged program as undermining parental authority. Charges are often made that teaching children to think critically, make decisions, solve problems, and work in cooperative groups where discussion is encouraged, undermine parental authority by exposing children to ideas other than those accepted by their parents.

- **Is the program harmful to children?** Frequently a challenge will claim that the program involves some form of hypnosis or mind control or some other approach or technique which is claimed to be detrimental to children. This issue of "Is the program harmful in any way to children?" is a pivotal one. From both a legal and ethical viewpoint, school counselors have an obligation to "Do no harm." If any program is proven to be—or likely to be—harmful to children, it should not be used or should be discontinued if it is being used. The issue here is usually proof of harm or likelihood of harm. The challenger is in the position of supplying evidence to support a claim that the program challenged is indeed harmful. The school counselor and school system are in the position of clarifying that sound criteria were used in selecting the material and providing research and opinions of experts that support the effectiveness and appropriateness of the program or materials. To date, challenges to school counseling programs or materials have not offered any evidence, which has been accepted by a court as credible, that any school counseling program or material has caused any harm to any child.

Related to the four issues discussed above, Peterson and Poppen (1992a) suggested two important questions were related to challenges of school counseling materials and programs: (1) Who determines what school guidance materials are used in public schools, and (2) Is the role of the schools seen primarily as a place where diverse ideas should be presented and explored, or is the role of schools to be primarily that of transmitting local community values? And if so, whose?

The guiding principle for school counselors involved in challenges, which reflects the legal and ethical codes, has been and should remain "What is best for the children?" The aim of this book is to help protect the rights of children to receive a developmentally based comprehensive school counseling program which the authors believe is critically needed to help children to be successful in school, work, and in life.

Overview of Court, D.O.E., and School Board Decisions

In order for counselors to determine if a challenge to a program has validity, counselors need to be aware of court and U.S. Department of Education decisions, school board rulings, and educational research. A brief overview of court, D.O.E., and school board rulings follows. Educational research is presented in Chapter 2.

Decisions by U.S. Courts and U.S. Department of Education

No court decisions to date have supported the claims that school counseling materials or programs were illegal or harmful. A 1985 court case that focused on the four issues listed above which also involved a self-esteem program, "Project Self-Esteem," is of particular importance. Project Self-Esteem has many similarities to other widely used counseling materials such as *PUMSY In Pursuit of Excellence* by Jill Anderson, and *Developing Understanding of Self and Others (DUSO)* by Don Dinkmeyer. In this case (*Capistrano Parents Committee for Academic Freedom v. Capistrano Unified School District*, December, 1985), the Superior Court of the State of California for the County of Orange found in favor of the defendant (the school district) and concluded that the Project Self-Esteem program: (1) is not a religious program, does not constitute advancement of religion, and does not violate the establishment clause of the United States Constitution; (2) does not involve psychological treatment; and (3) does not violate the right to privacy.

The Hatch Amendment and the First Amendment to the U.S. Constitution are the legal keys to challenges to school counseling programs. Kaplan and Geoffroy (1987), in two articles, gave an excellent history of the Hatch Amendment (which is most frequently used as the legal grounds for challenging programs) and First Amendment issues related to censorship and school counseling programs.

The Hatch Amendment, also known as the Protection of Pupil Rights Amendment, requires parental permission before students involved in federally-funded programs can be psychologically or psychiatrically tested or treated. In order for the Hatch Amendment to apply to a curriculum challenge, three issues must be present: (1) the materials or program must be fully supported by federal funds, (2) the materials or program must be experimental, and (3) the materials or program's primary purpose of testing or treatment must be to reveal personal information about one or more of the following categories as they relate to the student or the student's family: a) Political affiliations; b) potentially embarrassing mental or psychological problems; c) sexual behavior and attitudes; d) illegal, antisocial, self-incriminating, and demeaning behavior; e) income; f) legally-privileged relationships; or g) critical appraisals of family members. If *any* of the three issues listed above are *not* present, then the Hatch Amendment does not apply.

Regarding the First Amendment issue of freedom of religion, Kaplan and Geoffroy (1987) concluded, after their review of pertinent court cases, that "the First Amendment protects students' rights to receive information at school. Parents challenging 'objectionable' curricula, such as sex education or affective-psychological education, would not find judicial relief if they sought to restrict a child's access to information and ideas."

Kaplan and Geoffroy also reported that several complaints regarding the issues listed above have been filed with the United States Department of Education, and all have been judged invalid. More recently the United States Department of Education reported no new complaints related to counseling material during 1992.

A summary of court rulings regarding censorship issues for the years 1982-1992 follows.

Highlights of Censors in the Courts:
1982 - 1992

1982-83—*Board of Educ. v. Pico*, 457 U.S. 853 (1982)

The Supreme Court held that although local school boards have great discretion in running the schools and establishing curricula, they may not remove books from school libraries in order to deny students access to ideas.

1984-85—*Grove v. Mead School Dist.*, 753 F.2d 1528 (9th cir. 1985)

A federal appeals court rejected an attempt supported by the Washington Moral Majority to force a school board to remove *The Learning Tree* from its literature curriculum, dismissing the claim that the book inhibited their religion and advanced the religion of secular humanism.

1985-86—*Mozert v. Board of Educ.*, 827 F.2d 1058 (6th Cir. 1987)

A federal district court ruled that fundamentalist students must be excused from reading a Holt, Rinehart and Winston elementary reading series in a public school on the grounds that it burdened their rights to free exercise of religion. The plaintiffs had raised more than 450 objections to passages in the texts, including an excerpt from *The Diary of Ann Frank,* a discussion of the scientific basis of tidal waves, and references to evolution. A federal appeals court reversed and dismissed the suit on the grounds that the use of the reading series did not violate the First Amendment right to free exercise of religion. The court held that no student was ever required to affirm or deny any religious belief, nor were students forced to engage or refrain from engaging in any act required or forbidden by the student's religion.

1986-87—*Edwards v. Aguilard,* 107 S.Ct. 2572 (1987)

The Supreme Court struck down a Louisiana law requiring a public school to teach "Creation Science" if it also taught evolution. The court held that the law violated the First Amendment's Establishment Clause because it required the school to conform its science curriculum to a particular religious viewpoint, thereby advancing that religious belief.

1986-87—*Smith v. Board of School Comm'rs*, 827 F.2d 684 (11th Cir. 1987)

Pat Robertson's National Legal Foundation backed a challenge to basic home economics, history, and social studies textbooks in the public schools on the grounds that they advanced so-called "secular humanism" and inhibited theistic religion in violation of the First Amendment's Establishment Clause. A federal appeals court rejected the claim, precluding the group's attempt to remove the books from the public schools.

1987-88—*Hazelwood School District v. Kuhlmeier*, 484 U.S. 260 (1988)

Public high school students challenged their principal's removal from their school newspaper of two articles discussing students' experiences with pregnancy and parental divorce. The Supreme Court rejected the challenge, holding that a school may regulate and censor the content and style of school-sponsored expressive activities so long as its actions are reasonably related to legitimate pedagogical concerns.

1988-89—*Virgil v. School Board of Columbia County, Fla.*, 862 F.2d 1517 (11th Cir. 1989)

Relying on *Hazelwood*, a federal court of appeals authorized a school board to remove books such as *Lysistrata* and *The Miller's Tale* from an elective course curriculum on the grounds that the works contain "bad language" and "offensive passages."

1990-91—*Hamons v. Willard School Board*, No. 3:90 CV 7604 (N.D. Ohio Nov. 30, 1990)

A group of parents backed by the American Family Association filed a court challenge to *Impressions,* a K-6 reading series, claiming that it interfered with their religion and promoted the "religion" of witchcraft. A federal district court denied their request for a temporary injunction requiring the schools to provide their children with alternative readings. The suit was later dropped.

1991-92—*Brown v. Woodland Joint Unified School District*, No. Civ. S-91-0032 (E.D. Ca. April 2, 1992)

A federal district court rejected a challenge, supported by the American Family Association, to the *Impressions* reading series on the grounds that the exercises from the series do not promote any "religion" of witchcraft or neopaganism, and upheld the right of the school district to select textbooks on the basis of educational criteria. An appeal is pending.

School Board Rulings

No complete listing of challenges to counseling materials or programs exists. The two best sources seem to be Peterson and Poppen's 1992 report and People For the American Way's (PFAW) annual report. PFAW's report has a state breakdown of challenges and outcomes.

Peterson and Poppen (1992b) reported the ways that 82 challenges to counseling programs were resolved by school boards across the country between 1988 and 1991. Of the 82 challenges, the school board halted or delayed the use of the challenged program 16 times (20 percent) and continued use of the challenged program 66 times (80 percent).

Table 1
Challenges to School Boards
Regarding Counseling Programs

Total number of challenges 1988-1991	82
School board halts or delays program	16
School board continues program	66
(six of the 53 required modification before continuing use)	

Two keys to successful defenses of challenges to counseling materials emerged from reviewing school board rulings. *Community support was one key.*

Timberline Press, publishers of the *PUMSY* program, reported four "major" challenges to their program in 1992. A major challenge was defined as one that escalates to a high level of conflict and bitterness and continues for several months or more. The conflict deeply impacts the community, media coverage is extensive, a review committee is formed to evaluate the program being challenged, and a school board vote is taken. Of the four challenges, three had been resolved in January, 1993.

All three challenges ended with the local school districts supporting continued use of the *PUMSY* program. *All three district spokespersons cited strong community involvement and support for the program as a significant reason for the program being retained.*

Each of the three school districts have indicated a willingness to talk with other districts about curriculum challenges. They understand, much more than a district who has never experienced such a situation, what it is like to be faced with a major challenge. Information follows for those who wish to contact these districts.

- North Penn School District, Lansdale, Pennsylvania
  Director of Guidance—(215) 368-0400

- Oconee County School District, Walhalla, South Carolina
  Assistant Superintendent of Elementary Education—
  (803) 638-4064

- Charleston School District, Charleston, South Carolina
  Chairman of the School Board—(803) 722-1605

A second key to successful defenses of challenges to school curriculum appears to involve having and following sound policy for evaluating curriculum challenges.

A survey reported in *Attacks on the Freedom to Learn, the 1990-1991 Report*, which covers curriculum challenges in all areas, found that having a clear policy in place at the school district level and following it is very helpful in defending materials. *The survey found that when a challenged materials review process was in place and followed, 74 percent of the time the challenged material was retained. When no policy existed or where policy was not followed, challenged material was retained only 46 percent of the time.*

The school board information above relates to local school boards. One state school board passed an amendment of which school counselors need to be aware. The state of Alabama's State Board of Education, June 10, 1993, prohibited school personnel from using any techniques that involve the induction of hypnosis, guided imagery, meditation, or yoga. The problem seems to be in the board definitions related to these prohibited areas. Teaching stress reduction techniques, relaxation skills, and any type of guided imagery is now prohibited in Alabama. A copy of the ruling follows. This ruling is contrary to the professional literature, research, and many current recommendations from educational task forces which encourage the teaching of relaxation skills and guided imagery. A brief summary of this important topic is found in the next chapter, "Research Support for Developmental Counseling" under "Relaxation and Imagery."

**State of Alabama
Department of Education
Gordon Persons Building
50 North Ripley Street
Montgomery, Alabama 36130-3901**

Contact: Dean R. Argo

(205) 242-9705

MONTGOMERY, ALA., June 10, 1993—Following a public hearing at its regularly scheduled elementary/secondary meeting, the State Board of Education today adopted as amended *Adopt Rules to the Ala. Code Pertaining to Certain Teaching Techniques.* The amendment approves including definitions of certain terms in the new *Administrative Code* Rules.

290-040-040-02 Certain teaching techniques

(1) The State Board of Education is aware of concerns that certain techniques in some school materials or programs need clarification. The State Board of Education specifically prohibits the use of hypnosis and dissociative mental states. School personnel shall be prohibited from using any techniques that involve the induction of hypnotic states, guided imagery, meditation, or yoga.

(2) Consistent with state law, all school personnel charged with the responsibility of teaching students should take great care to emphasize that conduct prohibited by law is not appropriate in a civilized society. School personnel should also emphasize the consequences of conduct that is prohibited by law or that is highly likely to result in harmful consequences to the health of a person. Such conduct shall not be presented to students as legitimate options for their consideration. Nothing contained herein shall be interpreted as requiring the teaching of and/or about alternative lifestyles and/or illegal conduct.

(3) Local boards of education should make great efforts to identify parental concerns. Specifically, local boards of education shall, at a minimum, afford parents access to instructors and the opportunity to review the programs and materials to be utilized. For programs and materials not otherwise subject to state or local review processes, local boards should make every effort to seek the support of school patrons.

Author: Tazewell T. Shepard
Statutory Authority: Constitution of Alabama at 1901, amend 284,** 16-3-12, 16-3-13, Ala. Code 1975. History: New 1993

Definitions

1. **Dissociative Mental State**—Another way of describing a hypnotic state. It refers to the separation or isolation of mental processes in such a way that they become split off from the main personality or lose their normal thought-affect relationship. In such a state the boundary between the real and fantasy or illusion becomes blurred.

2. **Hypnosis**—A dissociative or altered state of consciousness, usually artificially induced, characterized by a heightened responsiveness to suggestions and commands, suspension of disbelief with lowering of critical judgment, the potential of alteration of perceptions.

   A common induction technique is that of progressive relaxation. This involves the serial or sequential use, in some combination, of the following: turning off the lights, reclining, closing the eyes, counted measured deep breathing exercises, counting backwards, alternate tensing and relaxing of muscle groups, repeating a single word or phrase.

3. **Guided Imagery**—Can be described with various terms or labels, such as visualization, visual imagery, guided imagery, or guided fantasy. Guided imagery is used as an induction or deepening technique of hypnosis/meditation. It involves the communication or suggestion, describing a scene in which the student/subject is encouraged to experientially participate, normally following a progressive relaxation technique.

   Note: Guided imagery, a common induction technique of hypnosis, should not be confused with the normal use of imagination.

4. **Meditation**—An altered or dissociative state of consciousness, often synonymous with hypnosis associated with or derived from the mystical traditions of the East, sometimes called transcendental meditation, normally induced by progressive relaxation (H. Benson's *Relaxation Response*), focusing on deep breaths and a mantra (repeated word or phrase).

   Note: This is not to be confused with secular meditation which involves alert, reflective, and cognitive contemplation.

5. **Yoga**—A Hindu philosophy and method of religious training in which eastern meditation and contemplation are joined with physical exercises, allegedly to facilitate the development of body-mind-spirit.

Greg Brigman and Peggy Moore

Organizations that Support Developmental School Counseling

The organizations listed below represent respected groups of parents, teachers, administrators, school counselors, psychologists, business leaders, government leaders, curriculum specialists, and others who believe that developmental counseling is an effective and helpful approach and should be part of a district's educational plan.

At the local level it is helpful to have a listing of district- and state-level groups which mirror the national groups that endorse developmental counseling. Presenting national and local research and national and local organizations that support developmental counseling to local decision makers can be very helpful in gaining and maintaining their support. Some of the organizations that publicly support comprehensive, developmental counseling programs include:

- The National Parent Teacher Association
- Lions Club International
- The National Conference of State Legislatures
- The National School Boards Association
- The National Association of Elementary Principals
- The American Counseling Association
- American Association of School Administrators
- The American Psychological Association
- National Education Association
- The National Dropout Prevention Center
- Association for Supervision and Curriculum Development
- Children's Defense Fund
- The American School Counselor Association
- The College Entrance Exam Board

Top Ten Suggestions for
Managing a Challenge

1. **Don't try this alone.** Connect with helpful organizations. This is a crisis. Consult with knowledgeable professionals at the local, state, and national levels. (See Chapter 7.) Use the Packets of Information A and/or B to inform your publics about your program(s). (See Chapter 6.)

2. **Be informed.** Learn about the tactics of censorship groups, their educational agenda, and their thinking. (See Chapters 3 and 8.) Be familiar with the language of the Hatch Amendment and the First Amendment so that you will be able to respond to the challengers with confidence when you are accused of violating these federal rulings. (See Chapter 5.)

3. **Make sure district policies are in place** in the following areas and that they are followed:

   A. Academic Freedom

   B. Guidance

   C. Request for Reconsideration of Curriculum Materials

   (See Chapters 4 and 5.)

4. **Inform and update your decision makers** during the process so they will be well informed as they respond to concerned citizens. They need to know that the materials are appropriate and safe, and they also need to know the level of support for your program. (See Chapters 2 and 6.) They also need to know about the groups behind the challenge. (See Chapter 3.)

5. **Inform your community early in the process.** Encourage the involvement of community support groups by sharing information about your guidance programs. If parent support groups understand your guidance program's mission and how your goals and objectives directly relate to that mission, they will support your efforts in numerous ways. Help parents network to mobilize support early in the process. (See Chapter 6.)

6. **Have local and state chapters of business, parent, and professional organizations write letters of support** that you can include with the support of their national counterparts. Start with elementary principals and teacher groups. (See Chapters 2, 4, and 6.)

Greg Brigman and Peggy Moore

7. **Involve the local media.** Invite an open-minded local media person to talk with you about your local guidance program and invite that person to come to your school to observe. Determine which national censorship groups are providing information or speakers, and provide the media with information about the educational agenda of these groups. Generally speaking, the media favors academic freedom, especially if they understand your goals and objectives and how they align with state, regional, and national goals. (See Chapter 6.)

8. Counseling techniques, programs, and counselors themselves will be accused of various things (illegally using psychiatry, violating the Hatch Amendment, teaching a religion, teaching children they don't need family or God, using Far Eastern mysticism, etc.) *It is important to ask for evidence/proof and to be ready with responses.* (See Chapter 5.)

9. The challengers will present "facts" that they claim prove their accusations are true, *i.e., PUMSY* has been banned in the state of _____, no child has ever been helped that has gone through a school drug program, and so forth. *Always verify these so-called "facts"* by calling the source, i.e., State Guidance Director, parent of child who was "harmed," and so forth. Most of the time the "facts" are not true, but you need to confirm and respond with the truth.

10. It is important to remain calm and respond to questions and accusations in the same manner, even when others exhibit impulsive behavior and believe materials/speeches from accusers without checking for accuracy. When the actions of some of the public are out of control, *it is important that you demonstrate stability and respond in an informed and confident manner.*

Summary

It is essential for school counselors to educate their publics as to the benefits to students, parents, and teachers of developmental guidance and counseling programs. This process should be systematic and ongoing and should directly tie the learning goals of the district, state, and nation to the objectives of the counseling program.

When a challenge to a counseling program or materials occurs, it is important to address the challenge in a cohesive and professional manner that reflects school board policy. The school counselor must take the lead in bringing to light the key issues involved in the challenge and how the courts, D.O.E., school boards across the country, and various national parent and education organizations have addressed these issues. It is imperative that the decision makers in a school district and the community be provided information as to the research support behind the challenged program, the broad-based support for developmental guidance and counseling and the agenda behind many of the national groups supporting challenges to school counseling programs.

The remainder of this book is aimed at helping school counselors communicate the importance and appropriateness of developmental school guidance and counseling. School counselors must be effective in letting their publics know how central guidance and counseling are to developing students into effective learners, workers, and citizens. It must be clear that school counselors do not provide therapy and do not try to usurp parental roles, but instead use an educational approach to teaching key skills and information tied directly to district educational goals.

Chapter 2

Research Support for Developmental Counseling

- Developmental Counseling
- Self-Esteem
- Affective Education
- Relaxation and Imagery
- Thinking Skills and Cooperative Learning
- *PUMSY In Pursuit of Excellence*
- *DUSO: Developing Understanding of Self and Others*
- *Quest*
- Guidelines from U.S. Department of Labor and National Education Organizations

Greg Brigman and Peggy Moore

Chapter 2

Research Support for Developmental Counseling

Decision makers in public education need to know the research support or lack of support for various curriculum, programs, and materials in order to fairly evaluate the merits of challenges. School counselors need to be aware of and provide the research support for the kinds of programs and materials used in developmental guidance and counseling. Communicating how the programs/materials used support the most current research, guidelines, and standards is an important educational function for school counselors. No one can do this job for us. It is our responsibility. The good news is that there is a tremendous body of research supporting developmental school guidance and counseling. For most parents in most communities, the more they know about the effectiveness of school counselors in helping children become effective learners and citizens, the more they will support school counseling.

The research summaries presented in this section are categorized under headings related to developmental counseling. The headings of developmental counseling, self-esteem, affective education, relaxation and imagery, thinking skills and cooperative learning, *PUMSY, DUSO, Quest,* and guidelines from U.S. Department of Labor and national education organizations were selected for two reasons. First, they provide a manageable system of organizing an enormous body of research and second, they provide a reference system tied to the program areas most frequently challenged.

Most of the summaries that follow are of large studies or reviews of research which offer a picture of the trends over time on a particular topic. From a scientific perspective there is more faith in conclusions reached after repeated studies over periods of time involving large numbers of people than in conclusions based on one or two findings. Challengers to school counseling programs frequently present a single research article as proof that a particular approach is not effective. Counselors who know their research are in a position to point out that one study may be out of the mainstream of published research.

In addition to being aware of the research on various components of developmental counseling, it is recommended that the school counselor follow these guidelines: (1) the program is based on sound developmental guidance and counseling principles, (2) the selection of the material or program follows recognized standards (i.e., state and local guidelines), and (3) the counselor using the materials or program follows the ethical guidelines of the American School Counselor Association.

In compiling this review of research supporting developmental school counseling and counseling-related programs, computerized and manual searches were conducted of indexes to counseling and educational research journals and ERIC documents from the 1970s through January, 1993, giving special attention to empirical studies. Only studies published in refereed journals were included. Summary statements of research articles under the topics listed under 'What's Under Fire? (Chapter 1) follow. These summary statements are representative of the published literature. This research summary does not represent an exhaustive search of all the professional research literature.

Developmental Counseling

Two important questions need to be addressed: (1) Why provide research supporting developmental guidance and counseling? (2) Are the critics challenging developmental guidance and counseling or just specific commercial programs and particular techniques?

It is important to note that the most frequently challenged programs (*PUMSY, DUSO, Positive Action,* and *Quest*) contain many of the goal areas of a developmental counseling program such as decision making, problem solving, understanding feelings, social skills and self-esteem. Therefore, an attack on one of these programs is frequently an attack on developmental guidance and counseling. When a challenge occurs, school counselors need to evaluate which guidance and counseling goals are effected and then decide if it is appropriate to include research supportive of developmental counseling in general in their information packet to key groups.

It should be noted that many of the form letters used by challengers call into question the entire area of classroom guidance. Careful consideration should be given to the literature used by challengers and not just the current target of the challenge. Developmental counseling programs teach children the skills and knowledge needed for healthy development and academic success. Developmental counseling is linked to reducing school failure and reducing school dropouts.

- Borders and Drury (1992) provided an overview of thirty years of empirical evidence pertaining to comprehensive school counseling. Borders and Drury found substantial evidence that school counseling had positive influences on factors related to educational development, including classroom behavior, attitudes toward school, school attendance, and decision making. Two of the key findings in the research literature review included: (1) there is general consensus concerning interventions that should be included in a comprehensive, developmental school counseling program (these interventions include individual and small group counseling, classroom guidance, and consultation with parents and teachers), and (2) individual and small group counseling, classroom guidance and consultation contribute directly to students' academic success, and improved behavior and attitudes toward school.

- A meta-analysis of 40 studies conducted between 1971 and 1982 found substantial empirical evidence that developmentally-based programs promote students' development and academic success (Baker, Swisher, Nadenicheck, & Popowicz, 1984).

- The United States Office of Education reported that there are 47 percent fewer dropouts and 50 percent fewer grade failures in high school when students had comprehensive developmental counseling in their elementary schools (American School Counselor Association, 1979, 1981).

- Cartledge and Milburn (1978) found in their extensive review of research literature that for elementary school children the ability to pay attention, listen and understand, ask questions to clarify meaning, follow directions, and get along with others were the most predictive traits of long-term school success. Developmental counseling focuses on these and related skills through classroom guidance and group counseling.

- Wehlage and Rutter (1986), in their review of factors leading to school dropouts, concluded that self-esteem and other psychological variables have been shown to correlate with dropout statistics.

- A longitudinal study by Gerler (1980) showed that classroom guidance programs have a positive effect on school attendance.

- Numerous studies have supported the premise that elementary school counselors have a positive impact on children's classroom behaviors and attitudes toward school, which may prevent them from dropping out (Gerler & Anderson, 1986; Cobb & Richards, 1983; Wirth, 1977; Deffenbacker & Kemper, 1974).

- Gerler (1985) reviewed 10 years of research from 1975 to 1984 and concluded that there was considerable research evidence indicating that children's learning and cognitive development was dependent on how children behave in school (Hoge & Luce, 1979), how children feel about themselves (Braun, 1976), and how children function socially (Cartledge & Milburn, 1978). These areas are important components of elementary school counseling programs which are designed to promote children's learning. (See Gerler, Kinney, & Anderson, 1985 for an extensive review of research on various domains important to children's learning.) In this same review of research, Gerler (1985) found that elementary school counselors have positive and significant effects on children's classroom behavior, students' feelings about themselves, and students' social skills, which were all related to students' academic achievement.

- Glosoff and Koprovicz (1990), in *Children Achieving Potential,* provided an extensive review of twenty-five years of research supporting elementary school counseling's effectiveness in the following areas: academic achievement/underachievement, dropout rates and behaviors, attitudes, and skills.

Self-Esteem

- Many researchers have concluded that there is a clear relationship between how one tends to view oneself and how effectively one functions in life tasks including school work (Caine & Caine, 1991; Coopersmith, 1981; Glaser, 1969; Brookover, 1969).

- Gurney (1987) reviewed the research findings relevant to self-esteem and children and made the following conclusions: (a) working on both self-esteem and academic achievement at the same time is beneficial to both; (b) a minimal level of self-esteem is necessary for learning to take place; (c) involving parents in developing and maintaining self-esteem appears to be crucial; and (d) it is important to plan for school wide intervention. A student's self-esteem is a vital concern for every teacher and is just as important as intervening to improve academic achievement.

- Purkey (1970) concluded that there is considerable evidence indicating a strong and positive relationship between self-esteem and academic achievement.

- Marsh (1984) and Wirth (1977) documented self-esteem as a responsible agent for general academic achievement.

- Caine and Caine (1991) found that what we learn is influenced and organized by emotions and mindsets based on expectancy, personal biases and prejudices, degree of self-esteem, and the need for social interaction.

- Nagel-Harmon (1989) found significant differences (at the .07 level) in the self-esteem of children who participated in the *PUMSY* program as compared to those who did not.

- American Guidance Services, Circle Pines, Minnesota has available a review of 25 research studies evaluating *DUSO (Developing Understanding of Self and Others)*, *DUSO 2*, *DUSO—Revised*, and *DUSO—2 Revised*. The review revealed that 23 of the 25 studies showed significant positive differences in self-esteem, general perceptions of self-worth, self-confidence, or social skills for children involved in the *DUSO* program, compared to comparison children. None of the studies showed any negative effect on children involved with the *DUSO* materials.

Affective Education

Affective education focuses on the emotional and social dimensions of learning.

- Gerler's (1985) comprehensive review of educational research related to school counseling found a positive correlation between affective education and cognitive development.

- Hoffman (1991) described affective education, or classroom guidance, as the instructional component of the elementary counseling program which is designed to promote children's social and emotional development and success in learning. It focuses on problem prevention and provides direct services to all children in the school.

- Baker and Shaw (1987) advocated the use of primary prevention techniques such as affective education for the entire school population, noting that all children in the school can benefit from and are entitled to these services.

- Educating the whole child requires attention to children's social and emotional growth as well as to their cognitive development (Hill, 1983). Affective education provides age-appropriate classroom guidance experiences to help all children experience healthy social and emotional development (Glosoff & Koprowicz, 1990). The curriculum for affective education is based on children's developmental and special needs as they progress through the childhood years.

- Caine and Caine (1991) reported that emotions and cognition cannot be separated (Halgren, Wilson, Squires, Engel, Walter, & Crandall, 1983; Orstein Sobel, 1987; Lakoff, 1987; McGuinness & Pribam, 1980). The implications for teachers include: (1) teachers need to understand that students' feelings and attitudes will be involved in and will determine future learning; and (2) because it is impossible to isolate the cognitive from the affective domain, the emotional climate of the school and the classroom must be monitored and needs to be supportive and marked by mutual respect.

- Carkhuff (1982) concluded in his review of 137 studies of living, working, and learning outcomes that affective-interpersonal dimensions are related to effectiveness in any human endeavor.

- Katz' (1986) summary of implications of recent research on children's development and learning stated that without minimal levels of social skills by age seven, students were at much greater risk of later dropping out of school.

- Aspy and Roebuck (1982) concluded that affective education (including interpersonal skills) was not a luxury but a sound investment. Aspy and Roebuck's conclusions were based on their research involving over 500 teachers and 10,000 students over a three-year period.

- Hadley (1988) confirmed earlier research with her study of second graders using an affective education program she developed. Her results showed significant gains for treating students in reading.

- Wooster and Carson (1982) reported dramatic improvements in self-esteem and reading scores after elementary age students were taught social skills and communication skills.

- See Glosoff and Koprovicz (1990), *Children Achieving Potential,* for additional research supporting affective education.

Relaxation and Imagery

Teaching children to relax and the use of guided imagery have been challenged as being hypnosis and as being potentially harmful. To the contrary, a report by Matthews (1989), professor of counselor education at South Carolina State College, synthesized research on stress and relaxation training with children and concluded that "relaxation learning emphasizes being fully awake, alert, and in control of the body." This report also made the following points:

- In the environment of young people, many intense life events exert pressure that requires the skills of coping or relaxation.

- High stress levels interfere with learning.

- Relaxation is a learned skill and requires time to learn and practice to maintain.

- Skill at relaxation improves performance of students in such areas as learning, test taking, social interaction-skills, self-confidence, self-management, lengthened attention span, and higher-order thinking.

According to Caine and Caine (1991), "There is a growing body of research on the power of visualization as an instructional tool (Galyean, 1983). Visualization is used for the purpose of helping people to relax, to attain a state of positive expectancy, and to induce creative imagination.

Far from considering it inappropriate for classroom use, the United States Office of Education, in a "Research in Brief" article (1987) titled "Eight Pointers to Teach Children to Learn," recommended the use of guided imagery to teach children important or hard-to-grasp information. Myrick (1993) provided a review of the literature on the use of guided imagery in education and made a case for its continued use. Myrick stressed the practical educational use of guided imagery as opposed to the therapeutic use and suggested teachers and counselors use planned scripts to guide students through school-related images and experiences.

Thinking Skills and Cooperative Learning

- A study by Education Testing Service (ETS) reported findings from a 20-year study of reading, math, and science testing. Two conclusions from that study were: (1) students lack higher order thinking skills of analyzing, evaluating, and communicating; and (2) students need more small group discussion, cooperative learning, and teachers who encourage active learning in order to develop higher order thinking skills (Mullis, Dossey, Foertsch, Jones, & Gentile, 1991).

- A review by Galbo (1989) of more than 100 studies on the effects of "cooperative learning" indicated: (1) increases in academic achievement; (2) more positive relationships among individuals from different ethnic backgrounds; (3) more use of higher order reasoning strategies and critical thinking skills; (4) improved self-esteem; (5) higher achievement promoted through cooperative learning methods rather than competitive, individualistic, or traditional learning methods; (6) increases in student motivation and retention of material which is being studied; and (7) involvement in elementary classrooms for most of the research.

- A 1989 Carnegie Council study called for more discussion, interaction, and opportunity for young learners to apply critical skills they currently lack.

PUMSY, DUSO, and *Quest*

According to Peterson and Poppen (1992), the three programs related to school counseling that are most frequently challenged are (1) *PUMSY In Pursuit of Excellence;* (2) *Developing Understanding of Self and Others (DUSO);* and (3) *Quest (Skills for Adolescents* and *Skills for Growing).*

Each of these three programs includes components indicative of developmental school counseling such as decision making/problem solving, social skills, self-esteem, and understanding emotions. Any defense of these or similar programs against a challenge should include not only specific research on the challenged program, but also research supporting all of the above listed categories. (See Chapter 2, Research in Support of Developmental Counseling, for more details.)

The following sections offer supportive information specific to the three programs listed above.,

PUMSY *In Pursuit of Excellence*

This program developed by Jill Anderson in 1987 is geared toward grades 1-4. A companion program, *Bright Beginnings,* is aimed at grades K-1.

According to Timberline Press, the publishers of *PUMSY,* over 17,000 schools in the U.S. and several other countries use this program with less than two percent (2%) experiencing challenges. The only research currently available on *PUMSY* was conducted by Nagel-Harmon (1989) which found statistically significant differences (at the .07 level) in the self-esteem of children who participated in the *PUMSY* program compared to children who did not.

It should be noted that many of the challenges against the *PUMSY* program focused on the guided imagery exercises. In 1993, Timberline Press published an updated version of *PUMSY* in which the guided imagery exercises were eliminated. Therefore, much of what was controversial has been removed.

One school system where *PUMSY* was challenged sought the opinion of a recognized expert, Dr. Bennett Leventhal, Professor of Psychiatry and Pediatrics and the Director of Child and Adolescent Psychiatry at the University of Chicago. Dr. Leventhal reviewed the program and the parent concerns and concluded the following:

1. The use of *PUMSY* does not constitute psychological treatment. It does not provide assessment or intervention for specific difficulties. Instead it is an educational program designed for classroom use.

2. *PUMSY* is age appropriate for grade school students. It is a potentially positive program for enhancing students' self-esteem, and its use of guided imagery is a safe, useful tool for educational purposes.

3. Parents need not worry about *PUMSY* breaking down their family values. There is a sound and significant body of research that shows that family values are basically stronger than all others. Use of this program should not impact on these values, and it would be almost impossible for this program to deter or override values set and modeled in the home. In fact, *PUMSY*'s home activities are designed in such a way as to promote active discussion of family values which is positive. Parents should be able to capitalize on this structured opportunity to openly discuss their ideas and values with their children through this program.

4. Schools which utilize programs to actively teach self-esteem and positive problem solving are to be commended. There is a strong body of research which shows that students with high self-esteem are more successful and do resist substance abuse more readily than people with low self-esteem.

Dr. Leventhal's full evaluation of the *PUMSY* program follows.

Sample Psychological Opinion

The University of Chicago
5841 S. Maryland Avenue, Chicago, Illinois 60637

To: Director of Curriculum

I am sorry that I have not written sooner to confirm my comments to you during our recent consultation concerning some of the curriculum matters related to your school system. My travel schedule and a number of other complications have caused this delay which I hope has not led to any inconvenience for you or your colleagues.

Please know that is was a pleasure to meet with you and to discuss the problems related to your program which is dedicated to enhancing self-esteem and a sense of emotional well-being in your students. As I indicated to you during that discussion, I thought that the concept was reasonable and appropriate for the curriculum in an elementary school. During our discussion, you asked me a number of questions and requested that I respond to them specifically in regard to PUMSY In Pursuit of Excellence. I shall do so to the best of my ability, hoping that they reflect at least the spirit, if not some of the detail, of our discussions.

First of all, I want to comment on PUMSY in Pursuit of Excellence as a program. As I indicated to you, I think it is a reasonably well-conceived program. Unfortunately, is it directed at a very broad age range and, as a result, some aspects of it are appropriate for first graders and some for fifth graders, but the program in total is not really ideal for any single group. None-

Greg Brigman and Peggy Moore

theless, there does not appear to be any danger inherent to the administration of this program. In fact, there appears to be considerable merit in giving this particular topic curricular attention. The idea of discussing matters related to self-esteem and a sense of identity is very important to children. Doing so in early grammar school, as a strategy for setting the stage for subsequent experiences which test one's sense of self-esteem and self-respect, probably serves an important preventive function and may very well be quite helpful to a number of students. A number of studies have suggested that self-image and the capacity to manage one's sense of self in a larger environment augers well for successful development. Since PUMSY seems to be directed to this end, I cannot see that it would be anything but helpful. While there might be a number of other curricular options which would direct themselves at the same educational goals, nonetheless, the concept is the same and certainly valid.

I do not see that the PUMSY program has any potential for disrupting traditional family values. In fact, the way the program is laid out seems to encourage them. Rather than setting the standards for how one should think and feel, PUMSY provides children with language and tasks which are designed to return them to the family to seek out solutions consistent with family values and family structure. Instead of being completely confined to school and setting the standards for the child, PUMSY allows each individual child and each individual family to find a way to manage their thoughts and feelings. In short, it is a very reasonable approach which enhances children's self-image within the context of their family values, as well as their community's values.

The program itself does use visual imagery, or guided imagery, as one of the instructional tools. This fancy name is used to describe a child using his or her imagination to understand how he or she might think or feel in a given situation. It hardly smacks of anything dangerous. This is a device that children use normally and routinely. That adults have adopted it and named it for the purposes of instruction really does not change the fact that it is something children will use even if adults do not encourage them. It certainly in no way reflects any techniques that could be considered "mind-control" or would be in the least way dangerous.

One of the questions that you posed to me was to whether this program promotes "new age concepts." As I indicated to you, I am not entirely sure what comprises a "new age concept." If it means that it adopts a certain set of values concerning promiscuity and indiscretion, I do not see that is any way within the realm of this program. Indeed, the program is fundamentally directed at children developing some sense of how they think and feel and learning how to manage their thoughts and feelings. Clearly, at times this means being able to say that you do not like certain feelings but it in no way engenders any disrespect for parents or authority figures. In some ways, PUMSY gives the child a sense of confidence that they can approach seemingly difficult problems without being overwhelmed.

There was some question as to whether this program constituted a psychological treatment or intervention. That could hardly be the case. The only reason one might construe this to be psychological intervention was because it was conducted by the school social worker. School social workers, particularly in this capacity, are simply members of the school's staff who have social work training. They are really not functioning in a traditional mental health mode. This is not by any stretch of the imagination a treatment program, but rather a program which recognizes individual characteristics and tries to help children enhance or strengthen their capacity for functioning. As I indicated to you during our meeting, I thought that this program could be equally, if not better, taught directly by teachers in the classroom with the support of appropriate consulting staff.

The question of whether this is age-appropriate for grade school students was addressed earlier. The concepts and the topics are certainly appropriate for school-aged children and, in particular, in grades 1 through 5. While the materials themselves might not be optimal for each of these grades, the topics are optimal for this grade.

You next raised the questions of whether the program's concepts or its methodology are potentially dangerous for children. There is no evidence that I am aware of in the literature anywhere that suggests that teaching children to improve their sense of self and improving their self images is anything that is harmful or dangerous. The techniques used in this program are traditional educational techniques and, while some of the language may not be perfectly suited for each of the children, it is not in any way dangerous.

There was some suggestion that this program might have a religious nature or contain the elements of the occult. I do not see that this has any religious overlays, be they in traditional religious terms or in the terms of the occult or Satanism. Indeed, the concepts of self-control, self-confidence, and the management of feelings seems to be something that pervades social and emotional development and, as a result, is often a part of the curriculum in secular as well as religious schools. These are universal themes in development and in human interaction. It is clear that they are not fundamentally religious and certainly do not represent any relationship with the occult. This program does have potential for being an effective and instructional tool. It seems to have very real potential for enhancing self-esteem and we know very well that children who have high levels of self-esteem and self-confidence, as well as a good overall sense of themselves, are less likely to develop psychological and behavioral problems in later childhood and adulthood. As a result, an effort to facilitate these areas of development should be a reasonable preventive strategy that appropriately belongs in the school setting. I might add that this is not the only place where they belong and, if they can be supported in community-based and family-based settings as well, then it is all the better. The PUMSY program certainly seems to encourage the use of family-based teaching as well as school-based teaching thus making it a program that has very real potential for helping children.

In short, it would appear to me that there is very little risk in teaching the PUMSY program. While there might be some room for improvement as there is for most school curricula, it certainly has no inherent dangers even to children who might have pre-existing emotional or other problems.

Once again, it was a pleasure to meet with you. If you have any additional questions or require further information, please do not hesitate to contact me. I certainly would be happy to discuss this matter with other members of your faculty or staff or with your school board, if you so desire.

Sincerely,

Bennett L. Leventhal, M.D.
Professor of Psychiatry and Pediatrics
Director, Child and Adolescent Psychiatry
Associate Chairman, Department of Psychiatry

With any school counseling program challenge, it is likely that the challengers will present their own expert(s)' opinions. It is therefore helpful to point out that the professional organization of which their experts are members, be it the American Psychological Association, the American Counseling Association, or the American Psychiatric Association, do not support the challenger's position. Neither does the research literature support their position. In other words, opinions that *PUMSY, DUSO, Quest,* or related programs are inappropriate or harmful are not consistent with the mainstream opinion of recognized professional organizations and the extensive research literature based on programs similar to these three programs.

Dr. Patrick Edwards, a clinical psychologist and assistant professor of psychology at Lander University in Greenwood, South Carolina, was asked by a school district in South Carolina to review the *PUMSY* program.

The significance of Dr. Edwards' remarks, which are presented below, lie in his analysis of some of the techniques used by challengers of the program and his discussion of guided imagery and altered states of consciousness.

Dr. Patrick Edwards
Assistant Professor of Psychology
Lander University

*I would like to thank you again for inviting me to share my opinions about the **PUMSY** package and the general challenge to such materials with your committee. As per your request, I have outlined the points I presented during the meeting. They are as follows:*

1. *That, while I am glad to see parents taking an interest in the educational process, I am concerned by what I see as their misguided challenges to a proven and accepted teaching package.*

2. *That I attribute part of the blame for this development to individuals, such as Dr. Twenty and Dr. Coulson. Through personal appearances, written statement/letters, and video-taped materials, these individuals and others spread stories designed to create fear and concern about programs like **PUMSY** and suspicion and mistrust of school officials.*

3. *Having studied the efforts of the above mentioned individuals (including listening to Dr. Coulson during his recent visit to Greenville), I have several serious objections to their messages and methods.*

   a. *They often use psychological terms in vague ways. The purpose of this usage appears to be directed at scaring parents and citizens ("Do you want teachers doing psychotherapy or hypnosis with your children?") rather than educating them.*

   b. *These individuals present themselves as experts, but they proceed to make statements that seriously call into question these labels. The undertaking of science is an accumulation of knowledge; no one study is seen as providing truth (the definitive answer). Scientists and researchers look at the "weight" of numerous well-conducted supportive studies before drawing conclusions about a program or hypothesis. In his writing and personal appearance, Dr. Coulson disregards this tenet and bases his beliefs/statements on several dated, isolated studies. By his own admission he ignores the bulk of the research literature, choosing to look at only those studies which appear to support his views.*

   c. *These individuals, especially on videotapes, will make statements like "any respectable psychologist" or "any psychiatrist would...." These are misleading statements which are meant to prepare the listener for a message by a psychologist (like Dr. Coulson) or a psychiatrist (like Dr. Twenty) who do not represent the mainstream views of either profession. If you want to know where these groups of professionals stand on an issue, you need to talk with members of your own professional community and/or contact either the state or national office of these professional organizations. (American Psychological Association, American Psychiatric Association, American Society of Clinical Hypnosis, etc.)*

4. *I often see the parents and other concerned individuals who raise objections to teaching programs like **PUMSY** objecting to what they label as hypnosis, psychotherapy, or "new age" religious techniques. These complaints are often based on faulty definitions or assumptions. In particular, at times*

these individuals will wrongly assume that because a psychotherapist might use relaxation or guided imagery in therapy or even in hypnosis, that any use of these techniques constitutes psychotherapy or hypnosis. This is a faulty assumption. Relaxation procedures and guided imagery procedures are used in a multitude of situations which do not represent either psychotherapy or hypnosis. They are used by coaches, business people, and ministers. Any local bookstore or library will contain dozens of volumes of "how to" books for adults and children which make use of these techniques. A person need not have any special training to use these techniques effectively and there is nothing dangerous about these techniques. They are important and useful skills and techniques for anyone to know and are appropriate for elementary classrooms. They are not the exclusive property of any profession or religious group.

5. *One area around which a great deal of confusion centers is altered states of consciousness. Some individuals express concern about teachers altering the student's state of consciousness. There seems to be an assumption that altered states of consciousness are somehow negative/problematic and give way to "mind control." Cognitive Science has for years been studying the area of "consciousness." We now recognize that consciousness ranges from what we call Normal Waking Consciousness to highly altered/different states such as Sleep and Dreaming. It now appears that most people spend their day moving between various different states of consciousness we call "Minor Altered States." These include daydreaming, absorption in a task (book, music, beautiful sunset, etc.), creative states associated with problem solving, relaxed states following exercise, to name a few. These states typically have a relaxing effect on people and are found to be pleasant and desirable. During these states the person is in no danger of being overly influenced by others, although they are often more open and receptive to experiencing the world in new (positive) ways. The relaxation and guided imagery exercises in **PUMSY** are designed to produce similar minor altered states. There is no danger of "mind control," and in fact the exercises are written so that students experience a heightened sense of control as they decide important aspects of the experience (whether to take or leave the basket, what words to put on the stones). One*

Greg Brigman and Peggy Moore

final note on this issue, if you talk with professionals about hypnosis (a technique for producing altered states), you will find many different definitions of what constitutes hypnosis. Some people might even call simple relaxation exercises "self-hypnosis." However, there is overwhelming agreement among professionals that persons in even the deepest hypnotic states **will not** *act in ways that go against their preexisting beliefs/morals. They will only do what they would normally do. We can not control people's minds or behavior with our most powerful psychological techniques let alone with simple techniques such as relaxation and guided imagery. We often use these techniques to help teach individuals to gain* **self-control** *over their level of emotional arousal and thoughts, not to "give-up" control.*

6. *It is my opinion that* **PUMSY** *is based on sound educational principles and is strongly backed by current research in the fields of education and psychology. I am very impressed with the* **PUMSY** *package. I fail to see any way that this package would usurp parental beliefs, a concern that I have heard voiced by some parents. Instead I feel its homework has been designed to promote a discussion between parents and child that will likely strengthen existing parental beliefs. I hope that in the years to come my own son will have the opportunity to be part of the* **PUMSY** *program.*

Again, I would like to thank you for allowing me the opportunity to share my opinions with your committee. Please feel free to contact me if you have any further questions.

Sincerely,

Patrick W. Edwards, Ph.D.

For more information about *PUMSY*, contact Timberline Press, P.O. Box 70187, Eugene, Oregon 97401, (503) 345-1771.

DUSO

DUSO (Developing Understanding of Self and Others) by Don Dinkmeyer was first published in 1971 and revised in 1982. It features stories and activities that give children structured opportunities to understand social and emotional behavior, to practice social problem solving, to learn to listen respectfully to the feelings and opinions of others, and to express their own feelings and opinions. The stories used are about situations children are likely to encounter in their everyday lives.

A review of 25 research studies evaluating *DUSO, DUSO 2, DUSO-Revised,* and *DUSO 2-Revised* revealed that 23 of the 25 studies showed significant positive differences in self-esteem, general perceptions of self-worth, self-confidence, or social skills for children involved in the *DUSO* program compared to comparison children. None of the studies showed any negative effect on children involved in the *DUSO* materials. The complete review of these studies is available from American Guidance Services, the publishers of *DUSO*.

Because *DUSO* incorporates many of the components of developmental counseling, any challenge defense should include research from Chapter 2—Research in Support of Developmental Counseling.

The publishers of *DUSO*, American Guidance Service, can provide very helpful material tailored to responding to challenges to this program. Two examples are: (1) an annotated research bibliography on *DUSO*, and (2) a flyer, "Tell Me About *DUSO*," which provides answers to questions frequently asked about *DUSO*. The information from "Tell Me About *DUSO*" is presented here.

Tell Me About *DUSO*

What is *DUSO?*

DUSO is, first and foremost, an educational program, recognizing the relationship between self-esteem and achievement. It has been used effectively in elementary school programs and as part of the educational program for other organizations, including churches, Y groups (YMCA, YWCA), and scouting organizations.

DUSO helps children:

- see themselves as capable and worthwhile people with strengths and weaknesses
- develop the courage to stand up for what they believe
- understand that choices lead to consequences and consider the consequences of their choices
- see ways in which they are alike or different from other people and learn to appreciate individual differences

DUSO addresses the relationship between self-esteem and school achievement by helping children recognize their own worth, increase their social awareness, and develop decision-making and problem-solving skills.

Greg Brigman and Peggy Moore

DUSO was published in 1971 and revised in 1982 by Don Dinkmeyer and Don Dinkmeyer, Jr. It features stories and activities that give children structured opportunities to understand social and emotional behavior, to practice problem solving in a variety of situations, to learn to listen respectfully to the feelings and opinions of others, and to express their own feelings and opinions. *DUSO* presents stories and activities about situations that children are likely to encounter in their everyday lives. Each situation includes a problem, the resolution of which requires getting along with others, honesty, and kindness.

Curriculum-related activities provide additional creative, imaginative ways to address each goal. Teachers can incorporate the curriculum activities into traditional subject areas to reinforce *DUSO's* objectives without requiring additional teaching time.

Why are schools concerned with children's self-esteem?

The early elementary-school years significantly influence the educational development of children. Research studies conducted over the past 30 years have suggested that few factors are more relevant to children's academic success and social development than their feelings of personal adequacy and self-acceptance.

A child with positive self-esteem is more willing to tackle new tasks without fear of failure, and is more confident about sharing the learning experience in a group setting with others.

Why is it important for children to learn about situations that may never happen to them? The story topics are typical experiences for many children. It is true that a child may not have experienced a situation—the death of a loved one, for example. However, it is likely that one or more children in the group has had, or will have, a similar experience. One of the goals of *DUSO* is to help children develop empathy for the feelings and experiences of others.

Do the activities in DUSO support a particular religious philosophy?

Although *DUSO* does not seek to promote the ideas of any religion, the desired outcomes of *DUSO*—self-worth, good communication, and respect for others—are in harmony with the beliefs of most religions and are moral values shared by society as a whole.

Because *DUSO* is a group discussion program, most *DUSO* activities are designed to encourage communication and discussion. Each story or activity is followed by a discussion in which children identify feelings and practice applying their own values when problem-solving a particular situation. Children learn to consider alternatives, in keeping with their own beliefs. They also learn about personal interaction and see that in any given problem, not everyone will use the same solution. When their classmates express different opinions, children learn to listen respectfully, even though they may not agree.

How does *DUSO* encourage sharing of feelings without infringing on family beliefs?

Learning to listen respectfully to other people, whether or not you feel the same, is an integral part of *DUSO*. In this way, *DUSO* activities provide a safe way to practice identifying and expressing attitudes and feelings, while at the same time respecting the child's values.

What is the purpose of the guided fantasy activities?

Children's play, from early childhood onward, revolves around fantasy. Fantasy allows children to be spontaneous and imaginative. In a *DUSO* guided fantasy activity, a script is read by the teachers, and the child creates his or her own image of the situation and visualizes—which is merely another way of saying decides or chooses—what to do. Children's own views, values, and experiences are brought to the activity; no outside philosophy is brought into the experience.

The guided fantasy activities in *DUSO* help children learn visualization as a way of planning what they might do or say if or when a particular situation arises.

Visualization is a tool that can be used in a variety of ways. For example, athletes are sometimes taught to visualize to see themselves improving a skill such as a backhand tennis stroke. Similarly, musicians use visualization as a way of mentally rehearsing a certain part of a score. Such rehearsal is also used in practicing refusal skills in drug education programs.

The situation presented in a guided fantasy is related to the goal or objective for the particular set of activities; for example, "to be willing to try new or difficult tasks," or "to act on one's feelings with courage." In other activities for the same goal, children consider what story characters might do or role-play a similar situation. In the guided fantasy, they imagine themselves in the situation and think about what they would do.

Greg Brigman and Peggy Moore

Each guided fantasy activity begins with a relaxation exercise, which uses a recorded script. The relaxation exercise was included in response to increasing concern about stress in children. It shows them a way to relax their body. The relaxation portion of *DUSO* is not related to meditation.

How does a teacher determine which activities to use?

A teacher chooses activities according to the program goals, the needs of the particular group, and the time available. The variety of activities allows for individual differences in children; some children will respond more freely to dramatic play, others may respond more to music, and others to stories. The activities for each goal are not interdependent; doing every activity is not essential to the success of the program.

Does *DUSO* belong in the classroom, or is it a counseling program?

DUSO has been and continues to be a forerunner in showing how guidance objectives relate to and can be incorporated into the curriculum. According to authorities in school guidance and counseling, the guidance program in an elementary school ideally will have a developmental, curricula portion as well as a consultative, responsive (counseling) model. It is the developmental, curricular portion of the guidance program for which *DUSO* was developed. *DUSO* activities can be incorporated into the curriculum, providing the generalized practice that is vital in a developmental guidance program.

Quest

Quest is a drug abuse prevention program with components for all grade levels K-12. Quest International, the organization that developed *Quest* programs, was founded in 1975 with a grant from the W.K. Kellogg foundation. In 1984, Lions Club International, the largest service organization in the world, made the *Quest* program the primary component of its international drug prevention efforts. More than 20,000 schools in 22 countries use the *Quest* programs. This widespread implementation has been due to the active support and endorsement of the Lions, the National PTA, the National Association of Elementary School Principals, the American Association of School Administrators, and the National Council of Juvenile and Family Court Judges.

The *Quest* programs focus on two main outcomes or objectives: (a) helping young people develop positive social behaviors, such as self-discipline, responsibility, and the ability to get along with others, and (b) helping young people develop commitments to their families/schools, peers, and communities, including a commitment to lead a healthy, drug-free life. To accomplish these objectives, the following skill/knowledge development areas are involved: decision making/problem solving, communication skills, and self-esteem. It should be noted that these skill/knowledge areas are key components of developmental school counseling.

A study conducted by Quest International Research and Evaluation Department (Quest, 1991a) involved 23 classes who participated in *Quest* lessons and 12 comparison classes, grades six through eight, that did not. The findings confirmed earlier studies that showed lower levels of use of beer, liquor, and chewing tobacco, higher levels of perceptions of harm associated with the use of drugs compared to control classes, and gains in knowledge of harmful consequences of drug use.

An independent research agency (Farley & Associates, 1989) surveyed a national random sample of parents with children in *Lions-Quest* programs and asked if they saw positive changes in their children as a result of the *Lions-Quest* program. Eight-eight percent felt their child was more aware of the consequence of drug and alcohol use. *Ninety-five percent rated as important or very important that schools should address positive youth development skills such as those taught in **Lions-Quest** programs.*

A 1990-1992 survey of more than 1,200 school principals (Quest, 1991b) showed that as a result of *Lions-Quest* programs, 69 percent of administrators believed students were less likely to use alcohol or other drugs. Sixty-four percent of administrators thought that students accepted more responsibility. Seventy-nine percent thought students developed more positive peer relationships and 95 percent believed the program supports the position that alcohol and other drug use is wrong and harmful.

In January 1990 the Westchester County, New York Commissioner, Steven Friedman, established a task force on social-competence promotion instruction for kindergarten through fourth grade students. Roger Weissburg, Associate Professor of Psychology and Director of the Prevention Research Center at Yale University served as chair of the task force. School administrators, principals, teachers, parents, and mental health professionals from both large and small, urban, and suburban school districts were included on the task force. The task force reviewed 30 programs. In addition to reviewing materials, the task force members made site visits to see the programs in action.

Lions-Quest Skills for Growing was chosen as one of the top three programs. A summary of the report findings follow.

Summary of Report and Key Findings

Lions-Quest Skills for Growing was chosen because it: (a) emphasizes interrelated cognitive, affective, and behavioral skills as well as prosocial values and attitudes; (b) provides sequenced developmentally appropriate instruction for kindergarten through fifth-grade students; (c) has clearly designed lesson plans that reflect attention to Social Competence Promotion (SCP) instructional theory; (d) highlights the importance of improving classrooms and school climate; (e) includes parent training and involvement activities; (f) has been implemented successfully in schools serving socioeconomically and culturally diverse students; (g) has the capacity to provide high-quality training and on-site coaching to teachers and administrators; and (h) presents some formal program evaluation data indicating positive effects on student skills and behavior.

Skills for Growing has many merits. The program is designed in an orderly fashion that makes sense and seems easy to use. The lessons are diverse, instructionally sound, and provide good balance of skill/attitude/information. The program materials are professionally designed and very engaging for students. The program has a strong theoretical base, working to develop both skills and attitudes. Adequate structure is also provided for students to apply their acquired skills to real-life situations. *Skills for Growing* also attempts explicitly to involve parents and the community in supporting program objectives. Furthermore, the program emphasizes the improvement of classroom and school climate.

Skills for Growing demonstrates state-of-the-art instructional methodology for 1990. The material was developed with careful attention to cultural sensitivity for a variety of racial and ethnic groups. The activities have been field tested and revised by classroom teachers. Each grade level guide seems appropriate for the grade for which it was designed.

The available evaluation findings conducted with pilot schools over a two-year period indicate that: (1) the content, design, and format of lessons work well for most teachers and students; (2)

teachers and student attitudes become more positive; (3) teachers perceive improvements in student behavior; (4) teachers and administrators respond positively to the training they receive; and (5) parents approve of the goals and objectives. The Task Force was impressed both by the research findings available to date and *Quest's* strong commitment to self-scrutiny and program improvement.

For a copy of the complete report submitted to the Westchester County Department of Community Mental Health, contact the Technical Assistance staff at Quest International, (800) 837-2801.

Guidelines from U.S. Department of Labor and National Education Organizations

The four sources summarized below have significant meaning for school counselors.

SCANS Report

First, the United States Department of Labor Secretary's Commission on Achieving Necessary Skills (SCANS) Report for America 2000 identified a three-part foundation of skills and personal qualities that will be essential preparation for all students. Part I—Basic Skills: reading, writing, arithmetic/mathematics, listening, speaking; Part 2—Thinking Skills: creative thinking, decision making, problem solving, seeing things in the mind's eye, knowing how to learn, and reasoning; Part 3—Personal Qualities: responsibility, self-esteem, sociability, self-management, and integrity/honesty. *Many of these skills deemed essential for success are both part of a developmental school counseling program and under fire from censors.*

NAEYC—Developmentally Appropriate Practice

Second is a position statement on Developmentally Appropriate Practice in Early Childhood Programs Serving Children from birth through age eight developed by the National Association for the Education of Young Children (NAEYC). NAEYC believes that a high quality program provides a safe and nurturing environment that promotes the social, emotional, cognitive, and physical development of young children (Hohenshil & Brown, 1991). These are the same goals of developmental counseling and are being challenged by censorship groups who want to eliminate all but the cognitive focus.

NAESP—Standards for Quality

Third is a set of program standards recently published by the National Association of Elementary School Principals (NAESP, 1990) titled *Early Childhood Education and the Elementary School Principal: Standards for Quality Programs for Young Children*. Included in the standards are a list of quality indexes that are important to school counselors. They include: (1) helping develop a positive self-image; (2) enhancing social and emotional development; (3) encouraging independent thinking and developing problem-solving skills; and (4) improving communication skills. These standards are also central to developmental counseling and are frequent targets of challenges to school counseling programs.

ASCA and Exemplary Programs

Finally, there are the guidelines from the American School Counselor Association and two books that summarize key components of exemplary school counseling programs. These three sources represent the most current and most accepted professional guidelines for school counseling in the United States.

Definition from ASCA (1990)

The American School Counselor Association recognizes and supports the implementation of comprehensive developmental counseling programs at all educational levels. The programs are designed to help all students develop their educational, social, career, and personal strengths and to become responsible and productive citizens. School counselors help create and organize these programs, as well as provide appropriate counselor interventions.

School counseling programs are developmental by design, focusing on needs, interests, and issues related to the various stages of student growth. There are objectives, activities, special services and expected outcomes, with an emphasis on helping students to learn more effectively and efficiently. There is a commitment to individual uniqueness and the maximum development of human potential. A counseling program is an integral part of a school's total educational program.

The Best for Our Kids: Exemplary Elementary Guidance and Counseling Programs

Gerstein and Lichtman (1990). Several hundred individuals including state supervisors of guidance, professors of counselor education, directors of pupil personnel services, leaders in professional organizations, journal editors, and other knowledgeable persons were invited to nominate programs that were, in their opinion, exemplary. After eliminating duplications there were 183 nominations of elementary guidance programs from 44 states. Each program nominated was described in a questionnaire. The questionnaires were then rated by a panel of 14 individuals knowledgeable about the field of elementary guidance and counseling. The panel consisted of three counselor educators, two elementary counselors, two elementary principals, two state department of education supervisors of guidance, one counseling association leader, one counseling education researcher, one professional consultant, one parent nominated by the National PTA, and one elementary school counselor in training.

Thirty eight percent of the 183 nominated programs were rated as "the best of this group of programs in terms of objectives, strengths, exemplary features, and innovative, unusual, or highly effective practices." This placed this group in a "best of the best" category.

The one common element among the programs rated "best" was that they were all developmental in nature and provide services to all students in a preventive model.

Comprehensive Guidance Programs That Work Gysbers (1990)

Norman Gysbers, professor of Educational and Counseling Psychology at the University of Missouri-Columbia, is a nationally recognized leader in the area of school counseling. This book describes eight model programs from eight states. Five program axioms underlie model comprehensive guidance programs:

1. **Guidance is an educational program.** As a program it has characteristics similar to other programs in education including learner outcomes, activities, and processes to assist learners to achieve outcomes, professionally certified personnel and materials and resources.

2. **Guidance and counseling programs are developmental and comprehensive.** They are developmental in that guidance activities are conducted on a regular and planned basis. They are comprehensive in that a full range of activities and services are provided including classroom guidance, individual and small group counseling, consultation, and coordination of counseling related services.

Greg Brigman and Peggy Moore

3. **Guidance programs focus on individuals' strengths and competencies, not just their deficiencies.** A major emphasis in guidance and counseling programs is on helping individuals identify the competencies they already have and then assist them to develop new ones.

4. **Guidance and counseling programs are built on a team approach.** All staff have guidance responsibilities. The certified counselors are central to the program in providing direct services to individuals as well as consulting and collaborating with other educators.

5. **Guidance and counseling programs mandate articulation.** There is program continuity. Activities begun in elementary school are continued, as appropriate, in the next grade levels.

Summary

Whether counselors are gaining support for their programs before a challenge occurs or responding to a challenge, the clear message to communicate is that counseling programs based on developmental counseling principles are in step with the mainstream of educational research and the guidelines of the most respected professional organizations.

In conclusion, there is substantial empirical evidence that developmental school counseling programs are effective and central to the academic mission of schools. This large body of research accumulated across the country is helpful in influencing local decision making. However, as Gerler (1992) pointed out, evaluation and documentation at the local level will probably have even greater impact. A powerful combination in winning support is to communicate to local decision makers both the general, nationwide research and local research.

Greg Brigman and Peggy Moore

Chapter 3

What to Expect from the Challengers

- Far Right Organizations and Activists
- Organizations Behind Most Challenges
- Educational Agenda of the Far Right
- Tactics and Techniques Used by the Far Right
- "Hot-Button" Terms and the Language of Censorship
- Arguments from the Censors
- The Typical Censorship Scenario
- Unless Effective Action is Taken

Greg Brigman and Peggy Moore

Chapter 3

What to Expect from the Challengers

Far Right Organizations and Activists Involved in Challenges to School Counseling Programs

Debate about educational methods and instructional materials and programs is not new to education. Open dialogue between schools and communities, along with balanced debate regarding the merits of a program or materials, can and should improve the education process. School counselors as well as any other school personnel should acknowledge the right of parents to question materials and methodology. At the same time, school counselors need to systematically defend what they believe is beneficial to children.

It is important to understand that these groups are generally of two kinds: local interested community members whose children are directly affected by school board action, and statewide or nationally-funded groups who target school districts in an effort to establish a national agenda that reflects their beliefs (Morris, 1992). One indication of the widespread activity of Far Right Organizations comes from People For the American Way (PFAW), (1992). PFAW reports that self-esteem programs have become the new target of the Far Right and that of the challenges to self-esteem programs that were reported in the 1991-1992 edition of *Attacks on the Freedom to Learn*, 90% involved Far Right organizations, either through the use of their materials or direct involvement. According to Morris, the primary goal of these national organizations is to censor or reduce intellectual options/ideas available to students. These groups have low tolerance for students being exposed to diversity, thinking critically and independently, and understanding and tolerating different views and beliefs. The language of the censors suggests that they feel they are protecting all students from what they perceive as potential life-damaging information, and this is their mission regardless of the rights of others. What is at stake is the academic freedom of all students. Therefore, it is important to be aware of the goals and agendas of the organization(s) involved in a local challenge, and to inform school decision makers.

Organizations Behind Most Challenges

The following organizations have been involved in numerous challenges to various school programs. The organizations typically provide materials and newsletters that promote challenges and control of public schools being placed in the hands of Far Right religious groups. The names of the cities, states, and challenged programs listed under each organization indicate incidents during the 1991-92 school year where information or direct assistance was provided by the organization to support a curriculum challenge (People For the American Way, 1992a).

- **American Family Association**

  Don Wildmon

    Deer Park, TX (*Positive Action*) • Pasadena, TX (*Positive Action*)

- **Citizens for Excellence in Education (CEE)**

  National Association of Christian Educators (NACE)

  Robert Simonds

    Prescott, AZ (*Positive Self-Esteem, DUSO*) • Dos Palos, CA (*Quest*) • Mooresville, NC (*Positive Action*) • Tiffin, OH (*Quest*) • Bartlesville, OK (*PUMSY, DUSO*) • Hellertown, PA (*PUMSY*) • Fort Mill, SC (*PUMSY, Bright Beginnings*) • Galveston, TX (Positive Action) • Quilcene, WA (*Positive Action*)

- **Concerned Women for America (CWA)**

  Beverly LaHaye

    Bedford, IN (*Quest*) • Fortville, IN (*PUMSY*) • Galveston, TX (*Positive Action*)

- **Eagle Forum**

  Phyllis Schlafly

  > Dos Palos, CA (*Quest*) • Colorado Springs, CO (*PUMSY*) • Clay County, FL (*PUMSY, DUSO*) • Fortville, IN (*PUMSY*) • Andover, KS (*True Colors, Quest*) • Bolivar, MO (*Quest: Skills for Growing*) • Hunsburg, OH (*PUMSY*) • Galveston, TX (*Positive Action*)

- **Educational Research Analysts (ERA)**

  Mel and Norma Gabler

  > Dos Palos, CA (*Quest*) • Mooresville, NC (*Positive Action*) • Huntsburg, OH (*PUMSY*)• Galveston, TX (*Positive Action*)

- **William Coulson**

  > Dos Palos, CA (*Quest*) • Bedford, IN (*Quest*) • Fairfield, OH (*Tribes*) • Huntsburg, OH (*PUMSY*) • Deer Park, TX (*Positive Action*) • Galveston, TX (*Positive Action*)

- **Focus on the Family**

  James Dobson

  > Bedford, IN (*Quest*)

- **Indiana Family Institute**

  > Bedford, IN (*Quest*) • Fortville, IN (*PUMSY*) • Huntsburg, OH (*PUMSY*) • Souderton, PA (*PUMSY*)

- **The Watchman Fellowship**

  Craig Branch

  > Fortville, IN (*PUMSY*) • Huntsburg, OH (*PUMSY*)

- **The Rutherford Institute**

  Pat Robertson

  > Huntsburg, OH (*PUMSY*)

Since most challenges use materials from one or more of the above organizations, it is important that the public as well as school officials know which organizations are involved as well as the intent of their educational agenda. Encouraging the local newspaper to focus an article(s) on the organization(s) that is providing literature or that is directly involved with the challenge is one way to accomplish this awareness. In addition, sharing articles on these groups from the National PTA, National School Boards Association, or other mainstream education organizations is helpful.

Educational Agenda of the Far Right

Understanding the thinking and philosophy behind the rhetoric of any group seeking change is essential for a community in order to make informed decisions. The underlying goals in the actions and language of these groups suggest an educational agenda that reflects a narrow sectarian perspective where students are expected to receive information as passive learners. A good illustration of this philosophy is found in a quote from Norma and Mel Gabler of Educational Research Analysts (ERA) in which they state that "one reason that secular humanism must be censored from the schools is that it teaches students that they can make independent judgments and decisions" (People For the American Way, 1989, p. 13).

The goal of the public schools is to teach children to be independent and critical thinkers in a learning environment that promotes diversity, tolerance, and respect for individual opinions. Additionally, this promoting critical thinking and respect for self and others approach reflects the philosophy of business and industry, the receiver of the "product" (young adult) from public schools.

The U.S. Department of Labor Secretary's Commission on Achieving Necessary Skills (SCANS) Report for America 2000 identifies a three-part foundation of skills and personal qualities that will be essential preparation for all students. Part 1 includes the basic skills of reading, writing, arithmetic/mathematics, listening, and speaking. It appears that most Far Right organizations want education to stop here. However, the SCANS Report continues with essential skills in two other areas. Part II includes creative thinking, decision making, problem solving, knowing how to learn and reasoning. Part III includes the personal qualities of responsibility, self-esteem, sociability, self-management and integrity/honesty. Public schools are being asked to prepare young people for the workplace of the 21st Century.

However, there seems to be a direct conflict with the educational agenda of Far Right religious organizations and that of public schools. One difference is in curriculum choices. This impacts significantly on the school counselor's role when it is clear that in order to be successful in a global society, people must respect diversity, demonstrate tolerance, and allow for individual opinions. Without a good self-concept and the other skills and personal qualities listed above, a person is not prepared to fully participate in life (family, business, community, etc.). The school counselor's curriculum frequently deals with self-esteem and these skill/quality areas.

Robert Simonds, national president of Citizens for Excellence in Education (CEE), comments on self-esteem. Listed below are highlights of the strong difference of opinion that exists about what should be taught in public schools.

"Does God's word teach self-esteem? Answer me. What does it teach? It teaches that we are nothing and God is everything. The reason kids are in so much trouble is because they have so much self-esteem that they think everyone should serve their every purpose" (People For the American Way, *The New Target: Far Right Attacks on Self-Esteem Programs*, 1992, p. 7).

Simonds' organization has a goal of taking control of public education as his comments below make clear:

"When we get an active Christian parents' committee in operation in all districts, we can take complete control of all local school boards. That would allow us to determine all local policy, select good textbcoks, good curricular programs, superintendents, and principals. Our time has come" (People For the American Way, 1989, p. 8).

The impact of our school board elections is noted in a portion of a column by Judy Emerson in the *Rockford Register Star* newspaper on April 1, 1993 in Rockford, Illinois. It told of the results of such a scenario as mentioned above that happened in the LaMesa Spring Valley School District in California.

Poppy DeMarco Dennis is a teacher in the LaMesa Spring Valley School District. La Mesa is just south of Costa Mesa, headquarters of the national Citizens for Excellence in Education. Dennis now leads a group called Community Coalition Network (CCN), which was organized to counteract Citizens for Excellence in Education activities in most of the 42 school districts in San Diego County. The Community Coalition Network has been joined in its efforts by an ecumenical ministers' group, a voters' group and teachers' associations from throughout the county.

Most recently, right-wing religious candidates won a majority of seats on the Vista School Board. Right away, the new members set about trying to implement their agenda, which includes reinstating prayer in schools, teaching creationism, implementing abstinence-only sex education, and opposing any curriculum materials that the religious right interprets as promoting the occult. The "occult" includes fairy tales, mythology, and exercises involving mental imagery, meditation, and environmentalism.

The new Vista board is having mixed success, Dennis said, because of public outcry and legal or constitutional constraints. However, some books already have been attacked. The board is trying to implement an abstinence-only sex education program. The right-wing majority recently turned down a $400,000 grant for a program called New Beginnings, a food and medical program for children in kindergarten through third grade. The new board members don't like "welfare" programs. In an attempt to trim expenses, one board member proposed cutting girls from the honors academic programs because he said the girls were going to stay home and have babies anyway.

Communities have to be aware of what's happening, or be sorry later, Dennis said. The Community Coalition Network has developed a program it will share with groups on how to counteract efforts of groups like Citizens for Excellence in Education. For information, write to Polly Dennis, CCN, 4690 North Lane, Del Mar, California 92014.

Three School Board seats will be up for election in November.

You can get in touch with Emerson at (800) 383-7827, or write: 99 E. State Street, Rockford, Illinois 61104.

Tactics and Techniques Used by the Far Right

The following ten techniques are cited by the National Education Association (NEA) as typical tactics to expect during a curriculum challenge involving Far Right organizations. Modifications and examples are presented below to make them more applicable to school counselors.

1. Name-calling and/or personal attacks on an individual or an organization rather than dealing honestly with the issues.

   Tim LaHaye (Family Life Seminars) is quoted as saying "Modern public education is the most dangerous single force in a child's life: religiously, sexually, economically, patriotically, and philosophically" (People For the American Way, 1989, p. 3).

2. Scapegoating. Affective education is to blame for all that is wrong with education, with students, and with society.

Greg Brigman and Peggy Moore

3. Taking statements out of context to distort meaning.

   Challengers to guidance programs have frequently taken statements out of context to distort the meaning. One such example is the statement, "I am me, and I am enough," from the *PUMSY In Pursuit of Excellence* self-esteem program. A challenger wrote that the meaning of this statement suggested that the student need not turn to one's parents or teachers, and certainly not to the Lord for any reason. The actual meaning of this statement, according to Jill Anderson, author of *PUMSY*, was that a student is enough without drugs, the fastest car, or the prettiest clothes. The goal of the author was to bring children to the realization that being able to say "I am enough," is a key to self-acceptance and is at the core of a positive self-image. NOTE: This statement is not included in the revised version of *PUMSY*.

4. Deliberate misrepresentation of facts. (They tell us only what they want us to know.)

   One ultra conservative newspaper printed that the program *Developing Understanding of Self and Others (DUSO)* aroused so much concern in New Mexico that the State Legislature passed a resolution against its use. In reality, a phone call to the New Mexico State Department of Education revealed that the governmental structure of that state requires the passage of a Memorial which then puts the issue into a committee for study. This is exactly what happened with the issue of programs such as *DUSO, PUMSY, Quest,* and so forth. The issue was studied for approximately one and one-half years and dropped; no resolution was passed to prohibit their use in the public schools of New Mexico, as the newspaper article would have the reader believe.

5. Conspiracy theories; the politics of paranoia.

   Both of these tactics/techniques are used to incite fear and distrust. When challengers use terms such as "Satan's Plan," "New Age World Religion," "Spirit Guides," "Antichrist," "children spiritually seduced and indoctrinated," some parents immediately react out of fear rather than investigate the accusations as to validity.

6. Emotional exploitation; fear-mongering.
7. Exaggeration; gross generalization.

   One criticism of affective, self-esteem guidance programs is that they utilize the practice of hypnosis and meditation, which are supposedly New Age religious techniques. Sometimes associated with hypnosis and meditation are relaxation and guided imagery. The challengers generalize that because they have determined that New Age is a religion, counselors who use relaxation or guided imagery in their programs are violating the establishment clause of the First Amendment, which says schools cannot promote the practice or ideology of a religion.

8. Basing a claim, or a series of claims, on a false premise. An opinion stated as fact. If the initial premise is accepted, all arguments based on it are believable.

9. Manipulation of religion and patriotism. The assumption that anyone who disagrees with the Far Right agenda is both un-American and anti-God.

   The term "global education" is interpreted as crowding out studies of traditional western civilization and promoting a new religion for the world based on eastern mysticism. The fear is that global education promotes principles of a one-world government and the dissolving of national boundaries and patriotism.

10. Red-baiting. Any expression of dissent with national policy is disloyal and a sign of Communist or Socialist leanings.

    Pat Robertson sees public schools as especially dangerous. As he explained on his *700 Club* television program: "The state steadily is attempting to do something that few states other than the Nazis and the Soviets have attempted to do, namely to take the children away from the parents and to educate them in a philosophy that will ultimately lead toward Marxism, socialism, and a communistic type of ideology" (People For the American Way, 1989, p. 12).

For this information to be meaningful, match actual examples from your district's experience with censorship groups and the applicable technique(s) above. Provide a 1-2 page letter or memorandum which labels these tactics to help educate the public. An educated public is the best defense against censorship.

Be Aware of Far Right "Hot-Button" Terms and the Language of Censorship

"Hot Button Terms"

- Role Playing
- Stress Management
- Visual Imagery
- Affective Education
- Values Clarification Activities
- Self-Esteem
- Relaxation Training
- Cooperative Learning

If you are using any of these techniques in the school setting, you should be aware of: (a) the research supporting the technique(s), and (b) the appropriate use of the technique(s) in the school setting.

Language of Censorship

A collection of catch-phrases that become scare tactics are frequently used by opponents to school counseling programs. According to People For the American Way, the use of these terms is "an effective tactic for creating confusion and fear in communities across the country." All of these terms are used to oppose teaching children to think critically and independently. They also object to allowing for different views and beliefs and oppose children appreciating differences in society.

The terms are "used without any attempt at precision. Their very vagueness is their great virtue. They are broad enough to encompass most any subject, and are used to challenge any materials, methods, and ideas found objectionable."

The following terms are most frequently used by the challengers (People For the American Way, 1992):

- Secular Humanism
- New Age
- Values Clarification
- Invasion of Privacy
- The Occult
- Usurping Parental Authority
- "Negativism"

Arguments From the Censors

Donelson (1987) provided a list of common arguments presented by censors. The listing below is a modification of that list.

1. Why don't you present both sides of an issue?
2. Why don't you join us in trying to save our youth?
3. Why don't you use traditional methods and materials?
4. You remove or change books for "feminists." Why won't you honor our requests?
5. Why are you promoting dangerous ideas?
6. Shouldn't we have a right to have our children educated according to our beliefs?

You are encouraged to sincerely listen to concerned parents and citizens; many of them express their fear, confusion, and alarm based on heart-felt emotions. If you deal with their concerns in a calm, reassuring manner, you may be able to assist them in understanding your program and what you do as compared to what they may have been led to believe. Usually when parents/citizens have been given accurate information and allowed an opportunity to review the materials and/or visit the classroom to observe, they realize that your program is in line with accepted methods and techniques of a mainstream guidance curriculum. It should be noted that in order for you to respond with confidence, you need to be thoroughly familiar with your materials and how they relate to your goals and objectives.

For parents and citizens who exhibit a single-mindedness regarding this issue and are unwilling to consider information from you, it may be necessary to give them a Request for Reconsideration of Instructional Materials form along with a copy of your district's policy on reconsideration of materials through a review committee. Encourage them to complete the form and return it to the appropriate district administrator so that their request can be properly addressed.

Knowing in advance some of the arguments you are likely to hear gives you an opportunity to consider with your colleagues how you want to respond. Because being confronted with these types of emotionally laden arguments can be unsettling, we suggest you think about and write out your responses to these six questions and discuss them with other professionals.

The Typical Censorship Scenario

Following is the usual sequence of events that occurs when a curriculum controversy escalates and school personnel are unsuccessful in thwarting the barrage of allegations and rhetoric along with a list of likely consequences if effective action is not taken (Jones, 1990).

1. A district administrator or teacher receives an initial complaint by phone, a visit, or a letter.

2. Information attempts to resolve the concern are not successful.

3. A group of concerned citizens appears at a board meeting to express complaints and give demands. Often they are armed with legal quotes, pamphlets, video cameras, and prepared rhetorical statements.

4. Letters to the editor begin appearing in the local newspaper.

5. Flyers or notices are distributed throughout the community containing complaints, allegations, charges, and so forth.

6. Community meetings begin and at times feature guest speakers from regional or national Far Right organizations.

7. Board meetings become stages for hostile confrontations.

8. Newspaper and television coverage mounts, initiated and sustained most often by the ultra-conservative activists.

9. Certain administrators, teachers, or board members are singled out as the ultimate villains.

10. Materials Review Committee members receive intimidating phone calls and letters.

11. Board recall petitions are circulated.

12. Law suits are threatened (often initiated from both camps).

13 School funding elections are not supported.

14. Legal fees for the district accelerate.

15. New school board candidates, representing the Far Right philosophy, surface and are often supported by outside funds.

16. The confrontation recycles for about three years as new topics and issues are challenged.

Unless Effective Action is Taken

- Educational programs lose their momentum.
- Random, persistent charges will continue to undermine staff effectiveness and trust.
- School-community relationships begin to deteriorate.
- Frustrations and hostilities are manifested inwardly toward self or other staff members.
- Some staff will leave the district.
- Educators self-censor to avoid any more conflicts.
- The school board becomes a mouthpiece and power base for the Religious Right.

Summary

This chapter has described what can be expected when a school counseling program comes under the attack of one or more censorship groups. The major Far Right organizations and activists involved in the censorship movement were described including their educational agenda. Propaganda techniques used by censorship groups and a typical censorship scenario were presented. The chapter concluded with the likely outcomes to be expected if effective action is not taken to manage a challenge.

Chapter 4

An Ounce of Prevention: What to Do Before a Challenge Occurs

- ASCA Guidelines for Preventing Challenges
- Proactive Strategies to Build Support for School Counseling and Protect Students' Access to School Counseling Programs and Materials
- Summary of What to Do Before a Challenge Occurs

Chapter 4

An Ounce of Prevention: What to Do Before a Challenge Occurs

This chapter begins with a quick reference guide to preventing challenges developed by the American School Counselors Association. The remainder of the chapter offers proactive strategies counselors can use at three levels (state, district, and local) which promote understanding, build support, and protect students' access to school counseling programs and materials. The chapter concludes with a summary of what to do before a challenge occurs.

The chapter has two assumptions:

1. Sooner or later, a challenge to your school counseling program or material will occur. No matter what a school or school district does to prevent a challenge, the very nature of a pluralistic society that enjoys free speech is to encourage or at least allow criticism. This questioning can serve a positive purpose by requiring constant evaluation of curriculum and materials which ensure use of effective programs and practices.

2. By taking a positive, proactive approach toward involving teachers, parents, students, administrators, and community leaders in the process of program building, school counselors create an effective support base. This support base, built on involvement and understanding, is very important when challenges arise.

ASCA Guidelines for Preventing Challenges

An ounce of prevention is worth a pound of cure. Professional school counselors can prevent challenges to school counseling programs, materials, and activities by implementing strategies that promote understanding. The counselor that is prepared by being aware of accepted standards for professionals in the field of guidance and counseling is better able to defend program goals when challenges occur.

Establishing a strong foundation through solid school board policies and comprehensive developmental guidance programs/curricula assures that appropriate decisions are being made. Once the proper foundation is in place, the counselors can organize and implement guidance programs with assurance that national, state, regional, and local standards/guidelines/policies will support guidance activities.

Involving local and district guidance committees made up of a cross section of community representatives is one important process that can establish strong support for comprehensive developmental guidance and counseling programs. Conducting needs surveys and evaluations of guidance and counseling programs and sharing the results is another excellent way to build support.

The guidelines for preventing challenges below, written by ASCA, will be very useful to counselors. They are offered in three areas and can be easily implemented in the appropriate sequential order in which they are presented.

Prepare

- Read ASCA's position statement, "The School Counselor and Censorship," and ASCA's "Ethical Standards For School Counselors."

- Examine personal and educational philosophies as they relate to potential controversial issues in counseling.

- Be aware of counseling-related controversial issues, challenges and legal cases as they are reported in professional journals and popular magazines.

- Be aware of available resources and reference materials.

- Keep school and district administrators informed concerning relevant program materials, curricula, and goals.

- Ensure that the Board of Education has adopted a policy stating the process used for the selection and reconsideration of educational/counseling materials.

- Ensure that the Board of Education has adopted a policy concerning participation of individual students in counseling activities.

- Ensure that the School District has adopted a comprehensive developmental school counseling program and curriculum.

Organize

- Inform all individuals involved in the delivery of the school counseling program (including volunteers, paraprofessionals, and school staff) of the program's goals and philosophy.

- Use sound educational practices to establish developmental school counseling programs which are appropriate for the age and maturity levels of students.

- Select balanced yet diverse counseling materials and activities in accordance with school district's educational goals.

- Relate developmental school counseling program goals and activities to district and state educational goals.

- Follow any laws and school district policies which require written parental consent for student participation.

Involve

- Advocate for school counseling programs which contribute to the personal, academic, and career development of all students.

- Use advisory committees and other school and community groups to gain and maintain support for a comprehensive developmental counseling program.

- Provide opportunities for parents and community to learn about counseling programs and materials.

- Identify a core group of individuals who can form a support group should a challenge occur, (i.e., counselors, teachers, parents, administrators, religious leaders, etc.).

The ASCA Guidelines above offer a useful checklist of key ideas for preventing challenges. Following this section is a more detailed list of proactive strategies for building and maintaining support.

This section concludes with two suggestions that are keys to keeping your publics informed and preventing and managing challenges.

Once a counselor's program has been developed, making the public aware of the goals and objectives can be done through district and school guidance advisory committees, district and local school newsletters, and school board curriculum committee. Informing these publics with accurate information ensures that at least more than one perspective is being disseminated during a controversy.

Having a packet of information prepared is essential for informing the public of the correlation between national, state, and regional guidance standards and your guidance goals and objectives. This packet should be appropriately labeled by "national," "state," and "regional" standards for guidance programs and should also include the research which supports comprehensive developmental guidance and counseling programs. Having this packet prepared and available suggests that a counselor has a clear direction and is organized and focused in the implementation of a program.

Proactive Strategies to Build Support for and Protect Students' Access to School Counseling Programs and Materials

It is important for school counselors to be aware of proactive strategies at the state, district and local school levels which they can be part of and to take action on the strategies. Use the system of boxes and blanks below to check off accomplishments, clarify concrete next steps, and prioritize your efforts. Copying this list and keeping it visible provides a reminder of what needs to be done next.

State Level

Priority

_____ ❑ Comply with state guidelines on materials selection. If no formal policy exists, push for the adoption of appropriate guidelines.

_____ ❑ Coordinate local school counseling goals with state school counseling guidelines and state educational goals. If your state does not have a clear policy supporting developmental school counseling, push for one.

_____ ❑ Determine what state policy is on Intellectual/Academic Freedom and procedures for responding to a challenge to materials. If no clear policy exists, push for one.

I can see I need to _____

_____

_____

_____

My first step to accomplish this goal is to _____

_____

_____

_____

District Level

Priority

_____ ❑ Comply with district policy on selection of school counseling materials. If no clear policy exists regarding materials selection, push for one (see Appendix A for sample policy.

_____ ❑ Tie district school counseling goals to district, state, and national education goals.

_____ ❑ Determine what district policy is for responding to a challenge to materials. If none exists, push for one. Having a clear policy on procedures for the way challenges are to be handled may be the most important preventive practice to guarantee a fair review of questioned curriculum. (See Appendix B for a sample policy)

_____ ❑ Be aware of the procedures and make-up of the curriculum review committee. The purpose of this committee is to form policy suggestions, educate school and community regarding policy and enforce established guidelines. Be sure this committee educates the school board who is also on the front line of controversial issues. Part of enforcing guidelines involves hearing complaints regarding all educational materials (including school counseling). This committee should review only complaint cases that have gone through the local school curriculum advisory committee. The make-up of this committee includes counselor, teachers of health, social studies, biology, English (these areas commonly have materials challenged), administrator, media specialist, parents, clergy, public and mental health practitioners, and local media representative.

I can see I need to _____

_____

_____

_____

My first step to accomplish this goal is to _____

_____

_____

_____

District Level

Priority

____ ❑ Present the school board with an annual report of the district's school counseling program. Include not only what was done and how many served but some measures of effectiveness.

____ ❑ Have local media cover positive events, programs, outcomes throughout the year. Have counselors write articles and make presentations promoting school counseling benefits to kids.

____ ❑ Have a district policy which spells out which counseling programs/ services will require prior permission from parents.

____ ❑ Base your school counseling program on sound developmental counseling practices which have substantial research support.

I can see I need to _____

_____

_____

_____

My first step to accomplish this goal is to _____

_____

_____

_____

Local School Level

Priority

_____ ❏ Choose materials with care. Be sure they are educationally sound, age appropriate and that the selection process is in line with state and district guidelines.

_____ ❏ Tie school counseling goals to district, state and national educational goals.

_____ ❏ Keep parents, teachers, and administrators informed of school counseling program goals, projects, services, and outcomes. Use counseling newsletters, "counselor's corner" of school newsletters, PTA presentations, brochures, needs assessments, and annual reports to create a systematic flow of information about the school counseling program and its successes in helping children. One effective tool is the quarterly counselor newsletter where up-coming class guidance and small group programs are described and results of just completed programs are presented.

_____ ❏ Provide parents access to counseling materials at PTA presentations by the school counselor and during open house. Have a table set up with class guidance materials, brochures on the school counseling program, and parent education materials (which can be checked out). Let parents know you will be at the table to talk with them about materials and your program. Also, let them know that there is a set of the kits and major programs at the district office for them to review in more detail if they wish. (Local schools usually cannot permit parents to take kits or programs home for review because it interferes with the ongoing counseling program)

I can see I need to _____

_____

_____

My first step to accomplish this goal is to _____

_____

_____

Local School Level

Priority

____ ❑ Form a guidance advisory committee to help with accessing local needs and to provide input for program design. Include teachers, parents and students.

____ ❑ Educate the local guidance committee and PTA board about the value of the school counseling program. These two groups can become a potent core support team should a challenge occur. (See sample school counseling information packet in Chapters 5,6.)

____ ❑ Offer parent and teacher education classes. These classes create an excellent opportunity to build support for school counseling. This forum allows more time for parents and teachers to get to know the school counselor. They also learn that the school counselor is a knowledgeable and highly skilled advocate for children.

____ ❑ Be informed about censorship groups, tactics and helpful resources before a challenge occurs. Write or call organizations listed in Chapter 7—Organizations and Resources— for key materials that can help when a challenge occurs. Keep a list of personal contacts at each organization. In addition to these national resources, create a list of local resources that would be helpful in the event of a challenge.

I can see I need to _____

_____

_____

_____

My first step to accomplish this goal is to _____

_____

_____

_____

Summary of What to Do
Before a Challenge Occurs

In summary, when a challenge occurs, the school counselor wants to be in a position to say:

1. The challenged program's goals and objectives are directly tied to school, district, state, and national educational goals.

2. Regional accrediting standards require school counselors to provide classroom guidance, small group counseling, and individual counseling.

3. The selection process used was appropriate and followed district and state standards.

4. The program is based on sound educational principles.

5. There is ample research to support the use of this type of program.

6. There are clear indications of the programs being helpful and safe (No indications of programs being harmful).

7. There has been clear and regular communication to parents and teachers about school counseling programs.

8. The school counselor can count on key groups of parents and teachers for support during the challenge.

9. Parents, teachers, and students had input into program planning through the local guidance committee.

10. There is a clear procedure to be followed to fairly evaluate a curriculum challenge.

Summary

Chapter 4 presents the American School Counselor Association (ASCA) guidelines for preventing challenges. A structured checklist of proactive strategies to build support is given in a useful format for counselors to utilize individually or in a group workshop. A helpful, ten-point summary of essential information for responses/presentations is provided at the end of the chapter.

Chapter 5

A Pound of Cure—
What to Do
During a Challenge

- ASCA Guidelines for Dealing with a Challenge
- National School Board Guidelines for Dealing with a Challenge
- Nine Strategies for Dealing with Tactics of Censorship Groups
- Stretching the Hatch Amendment: The "Stretch" Letter and Sample Response Letter
- Responses to Twelve Typical Concerns of Challengers

Chapter 5

A Pound of Cure—
What to Do
During a Challenge

No matter how much work counselors put into preventing challenges to programs or materials, a challenge is still possible. As the previous chapter points out, efforts put into proactive strategies to educate the parents and community make facing a challenge much easier. Whether or not there has been a systematic effort to build support for school counseling, the ideas presented in this chapter can help a school district guarantee a fair review of a challenged program and insure students access to appropriate materials and teaching methods.

The section that follows presents guidelines in outline form from ASCA which provides an excellent overview to managing a challenge. The second section of the chapter offers more detailed suggestions which appeared in a National School Board Association publication. The suggestions follow a four-part model that include legal policy, political, and practical responses for a school board to consider. It is recommended that the school counselor share this section with administrators and school board members early in the challenge process.

The third section of this chapter follows a question and answer format and addresses nine key questions that school counselors may have when confronted with a challenge. The responses to the questions give important details for dealing with typical tactics of censorship groups.

The fourth section provides a copy of the "Stretch" Letter, a letter used by some challengers to try to stretch the intent of the Hatch Amendment. A sample response letter from the school principal is included. The last section gives specific responses to twelve typical concerns voiced by challengers to school counseling programs. The counselor who is familiar with these concerns and some recommended responses will feel more confident when these issues emerge during a challenge.

ASCA Guidelines for
Dealing with a Challenge

In the April, 1993 American School Counselor's Association's *The ASCA Counselor*, the following guidelines were offered to help school counselors deal appropriately with challenges to school counseling materials or programs.

A Win-Win Premise

- Acknowledge the value of parent and community involvement in school programs and the right of individuals to hold and express diverse beliefs.

- Be aware of the ruling of the Supreme Court of the State of California, *Capistrano Parents Committee of Academic Freedom v. Capistrano School District,* Case No. 46-02-32, that established that "a mere personal difference of opinion as to the curriculum which is taught in our public school system does not give rise to a constitutional right in the private citizen to control exposure to knowledge."

Prepare Ahead

- Have a procedure in place for handling complaints.

- Take time to adequately prepare (i.e., don't be pressured to discuss or respond immediately).

- Seek assistance from district personnel, professional associations, influential community and business leaders, and your personal support system.

- Verify accuracy and interpretation of information presented to challenge the School Counseling program.

Use Counseling Skills

- Communicate respect for parental role.
- Recognize legitimate concerns.
- Respect different belief systems.
- Employ effective communications skills (e.g., clarifying, paraphrasing, responding to feelings)
- Try to find common points of agreement from which to build.

Stress Positive Intent

- Emphasize educational goals and democratic principles.
- Address needs of all children.
- Explain specific concerns in the context of the total counseling program goals.

Manage the Focus of the Challenge

- Ask for specifics.
- Identify any hidden agenda issues and their source (individual and group).
- Avoid taking the challenge personally.
- Ask for clarification of inconsistent and illogical comments.
- Resist being intimidated or compromising professional beliefs.
- Be open and forthright when disagreeing.
- Express confidence in school staff and program development processes.
- Agree to provide a response to all specific concerns (e.g., follow-up meeting or written response).
- Call for help from others who have experienced a similar challenge. (See Chapter 7 for resources and organizations that can help when a challenge occurs.)

National School Board Guidelines for Dealing with a Challenge

When a school district finds that it must respond to pressure groups, it is important to develop responses at four levels: legal, policy, political, and practical. The following sections are from Morris' (1992) *Updating School Board Policies: A Component of the National Education Policy Network of the National School Boards Association*, Volume 23, Number 9, December, 1992—with permission. It is recommended that you share this section with school administrators and school board members at the beginning of a challenge.

The Legal Response:

You need to cover the following bases by securing a written legal opinion from your school district's attorney regarding the following: Hatch Amendment, First Amendment, academic freedom, and censorship.

Various courts across the country have upheld the rights of school officials to make choices regarding curriculum, textbooks, library books, and general subject matter. The overall message is that school boards have broad authority in and responsibility for deciding what takes place inside the classroom.

In *Smith v. Board of School Commissioners of Mobile County*, 827 F. 2d. 684 (11th Cir., 1987), the appellate court ruled that officials have broad discretion in establishing public school curricula as long as the constitutional values in the Establishment Clause of the First Amendment are not denigrated. In establishing whether forty-four textbooks on the Alabama state list of approved textbooks violated the Establishment Clause by promoting secular humanism, the court relied on the three-pronged Lemon Test, in which government must: (1) reflect a secular purpose, (2) neither advance nor inhibit religion as its primary effect, (3) avoid excessive entanglement with religion, to conclude that "use of the challenged textbooks has the primary effect of conveying information that is essentially neutral in its religious content to the school children who utilize the books" (at 690), and that "even assuming that secular humanism is a religion for purposes of the establishment clause (at 689) . . . mere consistency with religious tenets is insufficient to constitute unconstitutional advancement of religion." (at 692)

The fact that books are in conflict with individual beliefs does not mean those books violate the Establishment Clause. Indeed, if schools were precluded from using anything that offends any religious belief, "there would be very little that could be taught in the public schools." (693)

In *Mozert v. Hawkins County Board of Education*, 827 F. 2d. 1058 (6th Cir. 1987), the plaintiffs, a group of 14 parents, asked that their 17 children be allowed to "opt-out" of a reading course because the textbook series presented a systematic bias against their faith. The court held that "the requirement that public school students study a basal reader series chosen by the school authorities does not create an unconstitutional burden under the Free Exercise Clause when the students are not required to affirm or deny a belief or engage or refrain from engaging in a practice prohibited or required by their religion." (at 1070) The court also noted that under Tennessee law parents can teach their children at home.

In *Island Trees Union Free High School v. Pico*, 457 U.S. 853 (1982), a majority of the court stated a belief—but not a holding—that school districts have nearly unrestricted authority under the First

Amendment to make decisions about textbooks and their curricular material. The court was split on school board authority over library books. Since *Pico*, lower federal courts have limited school board authority over library books.

In *Zykan v. Warsaw Community School Corporation*, 631 F. 2d 1300 (7th Cir., 1980), the court stated that, in general, schools boards "have considerable authority to regulate the specifics of the classroom" and that "educational decisions necessarily involve choices regarding what students should read and hear, and particularly in light of the formative purpose of secondary school education, local discretion thus means the freedom to form an opinion regarding the instructional content that will best transmit the basic values of the community." (at 1305)

So, legally, your district is probably on sound footing with regard to its choice in textbooks, library books, and subject materials. However, politically and socially, it is almost impossible to insulate your district from controversy and pressures. Interest groups are likely to surface when changes in policy, school materials, or subject matter are introduced. Appendix C provides a sample legal opinion.

The Policy Response:

Sound policies on curriculum selection and instructional materials development will help outline a strategy for dealing with challenges to school board decisions. Make sure the following strategies have been considered:

Obtain a copy of your district's policy on selection of curriculum and materials as well as your policy on handling challenges to curriculum. Make sure district administration and school board members are aware of these policies.

Having a citizen advisory committee to aid this process will help build a coalition of advocates for the curriculum. If you choose to convene a committee, make sure it has a wide range of representation from both conservative and liberal factions, as well as professional curriculum experts and persons knowledgeable in the subject area being considered.

A period of written public comment on the proposed curriculum can alert you to the attitudes of special interest groups in the community and may give you advance warning of organized opposition to curriculum or material.

Having the materials available for public viewing at the school district office, the public library, or some other equally accessible place will serve a two-fold purpose. It gives those truly interested a chance to be involved in the process, and it provides a response to later challenges which suggests that citizens were unaware of the contents of the curriculum or materials.

A policy regarding complaints/and or reconsideration of existing curricula or instructional materials can be your most potent weapon against attacks on existing curricula. If you choose to create this policy, make sure it is very specific about the way challenges are to be brought. Many districts which have survived pressure group tactics have said that time was their most effective ally. An established process very often has the effect of dissipating a bandwagon mentality. Making opponents adhere to a strict code of behavior, as outlined in a policy, allows the board and the superintendent to keep control of volatile situations.

If an unexpected challenge should arise at public board meetings, make sure everyone follows the procedural rules for that meeting. Do not allow people to speak out of turn, yell, exceed the time limit, or bring any type of voice enhancement devices (e.g. microphones or megaphones), and make sure both challengers and defenders get equal access to floor time.

When first confronting these challenges it is important to listen and not become defensive. Stay calm and do not make any statements or decisions without first taking time to assess the situation. Find out more about the challenge, discuss the issue among your group after you have all the facts and, then, begin the process of resolving the controversy. If you appear unreasonable or dogmatic at the outset, you may galvanize resistance among community members who have not yet made up their minds. As Casey Stengel once said, "It's important to distinguish between people who really hate you and those who haven't made up their minds."

Appendix A provides a sample policy on selection of school counseling materials. Appendix B provides a sample curriculum review policy and a form for requesting reconsideration of educational material.

The Political Response:

If the organization/group you are dealing with has a track record of this type of political involvement, investigating past tactics and the likely progression of events will allow you to be better prepared to effectively deal with them. Local citizens generally are more responsive to negotiation and problem solving within the confines of the school setting. Statewide or national organizations generally have an agenda which transcends district interests and, so, are less likely to be open to negotiation. Bear in mind that all pressure groups have a constitutional right to be heard, and that there are times when material in the curriculum should be removed. Not all challenges are negative in nature.

When your school board decisions are challenged by pressure groups, the following recommendations may be helpful:

Be prepared by keeping abreast of which organizations are making challenges in your state. Periodic monitoring of newspaper editorial columns and metro pages may alert you to the presence of organizations moving into your area. Keep in touch with board members, superintendents, teachers, and counselors in nearby districts. If you are the subject of a challenge, make sure neighboring districts know about it so that they can prepare themselves for similar disputes.

Research the challenging organization's tactics carefully. Some use legal jargon to confuse and disrupt meetings, often incorrectly quoting from state or local guidelines as a basis for the challenge and sometimes using blatant misrepresentation of facts. In order to deflect this common strategy of misinterpretation and misstatement, you will want to make sure that you know how and where to search for the correct information.

Don't allow a group to "divide and conquer" your board members, teachers, or counselors. Remember you are a team and you have made a selection as a team. Designate a representative from your group (i.e., board, teachers, counselors) to field all questions on the subject under debate. If citizens attempt to contact others of your group, agree that each of you will make no comment on the subject and will refer all questions to the designated spokesperson.

Remember, when conflict arises, it affects everyone from the school board members and superintendent to the classroom teachers and students. Keep teachers, librarians, administrative staff, and classroom volunteers informed about your support for their programs and your desire for them to continue "business as usual," or advise them of your reasons for changing positions.

The Practical Response:

It is important to use a well-thought-out and executed approach to dealing with the effects of pressure groups that impose their agendas on school boards and school districts. Community involvement and support are critical in defending against pressure group challenges. Be prepared by knowing your strengths and using them to your best advantage. Know and cultivate your allies.

Opponents will come looking for you, so it's your job to go looking for community support before controversy arises. If you have included local citizens in the curriculum selection process, it is likely that your decision is in sync with the community. Therefore, pressure groups are subverting the process; it is then, your responsibility to protect the interests of the larger community and it is their responsibility to help you.

Contact the heads of community organizations which represent mainstream opinion. Ask them for their support if challenges should arise. This support should include communicating their supportive position via the established organizational network, gaining access to the local citizenry through television interviews, newspaper interviews, radio talk shows, and letters to the editor, and appearing at school board and other public meetings to express their approval for the curriculum, materials, or policies at issue.

Establish a citizens advisory committee to review new curriculum and programs. Do not forget to include local media representatives on your committee. Newspaper, television, and radio personnel not only report on what is happening, they are also citizens who live, vote, and send their children to school in the community.

If a school district finds that a citizen's review committee must be established to examine requests for reconsideration of instructional materials, a detailed 10-step process is given below.

A 10-Step Curriculum Review Procedure

1. Formulation of a curriculum review committee comprised of parents, clergy, business people, community service representative, educators (including curriculum experts, principals, school psychologists, teachers, counselors, and media specialists), and school board members. (Such an undertaking is not to be taken lightly; it is neither quick nor simple. This committee met every other week for ten weeks, heard hours of presentations and appeals, and read volumes of reports, research documents, and the curriculum itself.)

2. Charge to committee by the superintendent of schools to determine the appropriateness of the program/curriculum in question for use at the elementary school level.

3. Presentation of the program to the committee and distribution of copies of the program, in its entirety, to each committee member.

4. Presentations by complainants, both written and verbal.

5. Presentations by experts, including psychologists, psychiatrists, and attorneys.

6. Presentations by parents in support of the program.

7. Presentation of rationale and research concerning the program, including consideration of data to support or negate program claims that it helps in preventing school failure, reducing school dropout rates, increasing academic achievement, and/or decreasing problem behaviors.

8. Formulation of recommendations. To assist in accomplishing this step, the committee considered seven questions about the program/curriculum that addressed issues pertinent to its appropriateness for use in the district's elementary schools. These questions included how the program meets the education and counseling goals of the district, the adequacy of research demonstrating the effectiveness of the program, search for evidence of harmful effects of the program/curriculum on children, the program's legality, and listing of the positive and negative aspects of the curriculum.

9-10. Both of these steps are presentations of the committee's recommendations to the superintendent and to the school board.

Jones (1993), in an article titled "Targets of the Right" which appeared in the *American School Board Journal*, is another very helpful resource that offers suggestions and guidelines for responding to censorship challenges. Most of the suggestions mirror the points made by Morris (1992) which appear above.

Nine Strategies for Dealing with Tactics of Censorship Groups

The following questions and answers are attempts to respond to issues that have been frequently raised regarding effective techniques to deal with the tactics of the challengers.

Question 1:

Censorship groups typically flood school board members with phone calls and literature put together by national Far Right organizations. How can I ensure that board members get both sides of the issue so they can make informed decisions? There is so much information supporting school counseling and clarifying the agenda and strategies of the censorship groups that I'm afraid of overwhelming the board members with too much information.

Response: The following two packets include key resources that provide important background information needed by decision makers. It is extremely helpful to have an appropriate person present a summary of this collection of information in person to the board. It is also beneficial to share this packet with local media and other key stakeholders in public education.

Information Packet "A"

Parts or all of the following can be shared with key groups at the minor, moderate, and major challenge stages.

1. *Letter to local school parents from principal giving background information on counseling program and specific information about challenged materials. (See pp. 114-115 for sample letter.)*

2. *Brochure describing the school counseling program.*

3. *Local and state education goals and objectives pertinent to counseling goals and objectives.*

4. *Regional accrediting standards related to school counseling.*

5. *National, state, and local organizations that support developmental school counseling. (See Chapter 2.)*

6. *District policy for reviewing a request to remove curriculum materials.*

7. *Brochure (if available) or overview of challenged program.*

8. *Two articles from National PTA.*

9. *Two articles from National School Boards Association. (See Chapter 7.)*

Information Packet "B"

1. *Parts or all of Chapters 1, 2, 3, and 8 of this book.*

2. ***Children Achieving Potential** (Glosoff & Koprowicz, 1990) gave an excellent overview and rationale for developmental counseling as well as supporting research.*

3. ***Comprehensive School Counseling Programs: A Review for Policy Makers** (Borders & Drury, 1992). offered an extensive review of 30 years of research which provided strong evidence of effectiveness of various school counseling services including classroom guidance and small group counseling.*

Question 2:

How do we deal with our own colleagues who agree with the positions the Far Right has taken on educational and social issues?

Response: Opposing views on controversial issues all contribute to the vigorous and healthy debate of our society's free marketplace of ideas. But, try to distinguish between the issues themselves and the tactics of debate on those issues. We may not convince our colleagues (or others who disagree with us) of the rightness of our position; but, we can try to convince them of the wrongness of manipulation of religion and patriotism to ordain one's position (if you don't agree with me, you're anti-God and anti-American), unfounded claims, hyperbole, and gross generalizations.

Question 3:

Are there any particular signals within the community that should alert to an attack on the school district?

Response: Yes, several. When one of the "stars" of the Far Right, such as Phyllis Schlafly or Beverly LaHaye of Concerned Women for America, or Mel and Norma Gabler, appears in a community (on a radio or television program or at some community meeting), that's a pretty sure sign that plans are underway for some kind of assault on the public schools.

The formation of a "concerned parents" group and the attendance of leaders of such a group at board meetings, for example, signals a probable censorship attempt. We welcome "concerned parents" and wish that all parents would be concerned. But these particular groups, whose statements and speeches are almost always scripted by national anti-public school groups, are not friends of public education. Their purposes are not to help the public schools, but to discredit and ultimately destroy them. The only way you can tell the difference between an honestly concerned parent and an anti-public school extremist is by learning the tactics of extremism.

Question 4:

How should I respond at public meetings to misinformation being presented?

Response: Encourage supporters to attend meetings and ask questions and make comments. Have an information packet ready listing who supports these types of programs as well as your goals and objectives. Tie your goals and objectives to those of your district.

> *"I am concerned about the misinformation I am hearing. Much of this presentation has nothing to do with the curriculum here. What we are using is supported by district and state goals, and national organizations for parents, teachers, and business."*

Point out research supporting the program or type of program being attacked and that no research indicates negative effects associated with the program. Courts have been supportive of the use of these types of programs; no courts have rejected the use of this program or these types of programs.

Know the position of the National Associations of Psychiatrists/ Psychologists, and so forth. Point out that the challengers' "experts" are out of step with mainstream thinking.

Question 5:

The challengers frequently misuse educational terms. Do they not understand these terms, or do they purposely misrepresent the intent of the words?

Response: Always use simple, clear language. The following is a list of terms from the *Education Commission of the States* in their communications kit, *Communicating About Restructuring,* often used by those involved in restructuring. The "definitions" were given by individuals opposed to restructuring. You can see why it pays to use jargon-free language!

- **Critical thinking.** Learning to criticize your parents, question values.

  Response: *"I'm confused, aren't we seeing report after report from the business world saying we need to focus on this area of critical thinking and problems solving?"*

- **Experimental.** Anything that doesn't have hard data supporting its merit.

  Response: *"I'm aware of extensive research on the effectiveness of this type of program we are using here and would be glad to share this with anyone interested."*

- **Self-esteem.** Therapy, people (teachers) not licensed to practice psychiatry, performing therapy on kids, behavior modification, getting children to conform.

  Response: *"Our school district, the state department of education, the (NAEYC) National Association for the Education of Young Children, and the Association for Supervision and Curriculum Development, support a focus on self-esteem. We are not doing therapy."*

- **Cooperative learning.** One dumb kid learning from another dumb kid.

  Response: *"Are you aware of Galbo's (1989) review of over 100 studies which concluded that this approach helps academic achievement?"* (See Chapter 2, page 23.)

- **Working in groups.** Turning the classroom into an encounter session, "discussion groups," students don't have to pay attention to the teacher.

  Response: *"Most of the work world operates in small groups. Lack of skill in working in small groups is a very large problem. We need more of this, not less."*

- **Decision making/Undermining parental authority.** Learning that it's okay to take drugs and not being taught that it's wrong and illegal; shouldn't teach decision making.

  Response: *"This is certainly not what is happening here. We stress sound decision making which includes looking at negative consequences, and we certainly stress the negative consequences of taking drugs."*

Question 6:

When in a tense confrontation with a challenger(s), how do you respond? For example, when accused of using large classroom guidance activities as psychiatry or therapy, how should counselors respond?

Response: It is important to remain calm and not become defensive. It is very appropriate to respond by saying something like:

"I'm not sure what you mean by large classroom guidance activities, but let me tell you what I mean when I use that term. Large classroom guidance means that we go into the classroom to teach (your goals). An example of a large classroom guidance activity is _____."

If the challenger continues to misrepresent the educational terms, it is a clear indication the challenger does not understand the meaning. Drop the term; redefine it in simpler words with an example for clarification. If the challenger(s) continues to insist on that particular agenda, it is useless to prolong the issue at that point.

Question 7:

Sometimes the challengers will try to instill fear by claiming that a particular teaching technique has harmed students. How do we respond when we do not know if that is true?

Response: You can't defend or accept instances of which you have no proof. Respond by saying:

"Can you give me an example of when that happened here? Give me the name of the school, teacher, counselor, and so forth, and I will check out your information. I have not heard of that happening here, but I would like to find out if your information is correct, and I'll be glad to check on that when you give me the facts."

Question 8:

We have had some challengers ask our school board to pass policies that are broad-based in nature, (i.e., a policy to eliminate all affective education from the curriculum). How do we respond to such a request?

Greg Brigman and Peggy Moore

Response: Before a policy can be adopted, most districts have certain procedures for committee review and public review. At those times, teachers, counselors, and so forth would have input. It is important to stay current on the tactics of censorship groups in order to keep affected people (teachers, counselors, librarians, school boards, etc.) updated with facts. (See Research on Affective Education, Chapter 2.)

Question 9:

How can a community support group assist a school district during a challenge?

Response: One technique that can be used to highlight the attempts of censorship groups is for the community support group to print a monthly newsletter giving information on national censorship efforts, state legislative censorship attempts, and local censorship efforts by challengers at school board meetings. This is an excellent way to keep the public aware of censorship activity. An informed public can make appropriate reactions to censorship issues. One organization that helps concerned parents organize is the Freedom to Learn Network, P.O. Box 21352, Lehigh Valley, Pennsylvania 18002-1352. (See the sample of a community news letter in Chapter 7.)

Stretching the Hatch Amendment

What is the "Stretch" Letter? Some schools have received a type of form letter demanding many things they want from their child's curriculum.

The Stretch Letter earns its name from the fact that it purposely "stretches" the intent of the Hatch Amendment. (For more information on the Hatch Amendment and the school counselor, see Kaplan & Geoffrey, 1987, and Chapter 2). Its objective is to intimidate educators. Thousands of copies with the following lead-in have been distributed nationally by Far Right organizations. It contains errors and incorrectly identifies grounds for withdrawal of federal funds.

The sample Stretch Letter below and the response letter that follows are from Jones (1990).

Sample Stretch Letter

Parents: **How to Protect Your Rights**—Here is a sample letter (prepared by the Maryland Coalition of Concerned Parents on Privacy Rights in Public Schools) which you can copy and send to the president of your local school board (with a copy to your child's school principal) in order to protect parental and student rights under the Hatch Amendment Regulations effective November 12, 1984. This letter does not ask for the removal of any course or material, it merely demands that the school obey the law and secure written parental consent before subjecting children to any of the following. Parents are *not* required to explain their reasons for denying consent.

Name
Address
City, State, ZIP

Date
School Board President
His/Her Address
Anytown, USA

Dear Ms./Mr. President,

I am the parent of _____ who attends _____ School. Under U.S. Legislation and court decision, parents have the primary responsibility for their children's education, and pupils have certain rights which the schools may not deny. Parents have the right to assure that their children's beliefs and moral values are not undermined by the schools. Pupils have the right to have and to hold their values and moral standards without direct or indirect manipulation by the schools through curricula, textbooks, audio-visual materials or supplementary assignments.

Accordingly, I hereby request that my child be involved in no school activities or materials listed below unless I have first reviewed all the relevant materials and have given my written consent for their use:

- *Psychological and psychiatric examinations, tests, or surveys that are designed to elicit information about attitudes, habits, opinions, beliefs, or feelings of an individual or group;*
- *Values clarification, use of moral dilemmas, discussion of religious or moral standards, role-playing or open-ended discussions of situations involving moral issues, and survival games including life-death decision exercises;*
- *Death education, including abortion, euthanasia, suicide, use of violence, and discussions of death and dying;*
- *Curricula pertaining to alcohol and drugs;*
- *Instruction in nuclear war, nuclear policy, and nuclear classroom games; anti-nationalistic, one-world government, or globalism curricula;*
- *Discussion and testing on inter-personal relationships; discussions of attitudes toward parents and parenting;*
- *Education in human sexuality, including premarital sex, extra-marital sex, contraception, abortion, homosexuality, group sex and marriages, prostitution, incest, masturbation, bestiality, divorce, and population control and roles of males and females; sex behavior and attitudes or student and family;*
- *Pornography and any materials containing profanity and/or sexual explicitness;*
- *Guided fantasy techniques; hypnotic techniques; imaginary and suggestology;*
- *Organic evolution, including the idea that man has developed from previous or lower types of living things;*
- *Discussions of witchcraft, occultism, the supernatural, and Eastern mysticism;*
- *Political affiliations and beliefs of student and family personal religious beliefs and practices;*
- *Mental and psychological problems and self-incriminating behavior potentially embarrassing to the student or family;*
- *Critical appraisals of other individuals with whom the child has family relationships;*

- *Legally recognized privileged and analogous relationships, such as those of lawyers, physicians, and ministers;*
- *Income, including the student's role in family activities and finances;*
- *Non-academic personality tests; questionnaires on person and family life attitudes;*
- *Autobiography assignments; log books, diaries, and personal journals;*
- *Contrived incidents for self-relation; sensitivity training, group encounter sessions, talk-ins, magic circle techniques, self-evaluation, and auto criticism; strategies designed for self-disclosure;*
- *Sociograms; sociodramas (sic) psychodrama; blindfold walks; isolation techniques.*

The purpose of this letter is to preserve my child's rights under the Protection of Pupil Rights Amendment (the Hatch Amendment) of the General Education Provisions Act, and under its regulations as published in the Federal Register of September 6, 1984, which became effective Nov. 12, 1984. These regulations provide a procedure for filing complaints first at the local level and then with the U.S. Department of Education. If a voluntary remedy fails, federal funds can be withdrawn from those in violation of the law. I respectfully ask you to send me a substantive response to this letter (attaching a copy of your policy statement on procedures for parental permission requirements), to notify all my child's teachers, and to keep a copy of this letter in my child's permanent file. Thank you for your cooperation.

Sincerely,

Concerned Parent
cc: Ms. /Mr. School Principal

Sample Response to the Stretch Letter

Name
Address
City, State, ZIP
Date

Ms. Concerned Parent
Address
Anytown, USA

Dear _____(Parent)

The _____ School District has received your letter requesting that your child not participate in a number of school activities without your being afforded the opportunity to review the materials and to give your written approval. You refer in your letter to regulations which implement Section 439 of the General Education Provisions Act (GEPA) as the basis for your request. Unfortunately, you have received incorrect information about the intent and scope of these regulations. It must be emphasized that the Hatch Amendment, the commonly used name for Section 439, only applies to programs funded through the U.S. Education Department. Additionally, the regulations only apply to research or experimentation programs or projects and to psychological and psychiatric testing, examination and treatment whose primary purpose is to delve into one or more of seven areas.

Section 439 (a) provides that parents must be given the opportunity to review "all instructional material, including teacher's manuals, films, tapes, or other supplementary instructional material which will be used in connection with any federally funded research or experimentation program or project."

Section 439 (b) provides that no student shall be required to submit without prior written consent to psychiatric or psychological examination, testing or treatment in which the primary purpose is to reveal information concerning one or more of the following: (1) political affiliations; (2) mental and psychological problems potentially embarrassing to the student or his or her family; (3) sex behavior and attitudes; (4) illegal, anti-social, self-incriminating, and demeaning behavior; (5) critical appraisals of other individuals required by law to determine eligibility for participation in a program or for receiving financial assistance under a program.

Therefore, if your child is to be involved in a program or activity which meets the following criteria, we will notify you and request your prior written consent if: (1) the program is federally funded through the U.S. Department of Education and (2) the activity is a research-experimentation project or is a psychological or psychiatric examination, test, or treatment whose primary purpose is to obtain information in one or more of the above indicated five areas. If these criteria are not met, the Hatch Amendment (Section 439) Regulations do not apply.

Be assured that all activities which occur in our school system are directly related to the goals and objectives of the curriculum and have a distinct academic purpose.

If you have further questions, please contact _____.

Sincerely,

School Board
Representative

Responses to Twelve
Typical Concerns of Challengers

Although the following concerns of challengers and responses focus on the self-esteem program *PUMSY In Pursuit of Excellence,* the context of the responses would be applicable to any attack on self-esteem or other types of school counseling programs.

Specific challenger concerns include:

1. Use of mind-control techniques
2. Promotion of New Age Movement philosophies
3. Use of situational ethics
4. Use of guided imagery
5. Invasion of family privacy
6. Breakdown of traditional family values
7. Anti-Christian teachings
8. Decision making/non-directive education
9. Hatch Amendment violation
10. Secular Humanism
11. Hypnosis
12. "I Am Me, I Am Enough"

Issue 1—Mind Control:

Response • *PUMSY* does not utilize "mind control" techniques in the negative sense used by the complainants. It does teach children to control fears and anxieties which can interfere with effectively handling problem-solving situations. The program does control minds in the same general sense that all education controls minds. Through this program we teach such absolutes as drugs are wrong and there are appropriate times and ways to "say no."

Issue 2—New Age:

Response • *PUMSY* in no way supports nor belies any religious values. This approach to public schooling is consistent with the Federal Constitution, the 1st and 14th Amendments in the Bill of Rights. In addition, *PUMSY* does not utilize elements of the occult nor does it have students chant. It does utilize a little girl dragon as its central figure, and it does utilize repetition of concepts which is a standard and proven instructional technique for young children. Examples of this technique include repeating multiplication tables, spelling words, letter formation, and Bible verses. It is also a common theme in children's literature titles such as *The Little Engine That Could.*

Issue 3—Situational Ethics:

Response • *PUMSY* presents common situations which the students might encounter like being called names, failing a test in school, having to make a decision, feeling "down," and needing to "say no" to drugs. Students are encouraged to discuss how they might handle situations like this. Students brainstorm multiple ways to solve problems. Positive and negative consequences of their suggestions are clearly pointed out by the counselor. Students are given opportunities to practice their solutions. While some may consider this approach situational ethics, this approach is consistent with life and our charge to prepare students to effectively handle life's situations. Human nature leads children to imagine how they will handle situations. We believe that students who have a plan for dealing with problems, deal with them more effectively than those students who do not have a plan for success.

Issue 4—Guided Imagery:

Response • This instructional technique has 80 + years of acceptance in the educational community as a widely used and effective instructional technique. Primary students utilize their imaginations extensively and spend much of their time imagining. Guiding their imaginations is a better means than not providing structure. It is through this guiding that students learn the concepts which the program teaches. All instruction is guided by its nature. If it were not, students would not learn the objectives of the lesson, but mentally wander along their own paths.

Issue 5—Family Privacy:

Response • *PUMSY* was implemented in our schools in such a way as to minimize student disclosure of "family business." Activities in which students explored their thoughts and feelings were predominantly home-based activities designed to include the parents and to give the parents insight into their child's thoughts. Our intent was to involve parents through home activities to reaffirm their family traditions and beliefs. Classroom sharing was brief and no more invasive than other instructional activities which draw on personal experience. The ability to learn is tied directly to the prior knowledge which students bring to their learning and their ability to connect learning with their personal experiences.

Issue 6—Family Values:

Response • Family values are set by each individual family. At the primary level, students are so firmly rooted in these value systems established by the home, that it is not possible for a program like *PUMSY* to influence or break down family values. If the student's relationship to the family's value structure is so fragile as to be impacted by this program, the relationship could be far more significantly impacted by television, movies, books, peers, or any of life's other experiences.

Schools do not "break down" family values. Rather, they provide structured opportunities for students to practice their personal beliefs and standards in a safe and orderly environment with their peers. We encourage students to uphold their family convictions and not be swayed by peer pressure or other potentially negative influences.

Issue 7—Anti-Christian Teachings:

Response • Most educators would agree that young people should feel confident and positive about themselves. With this solid ground, children tend to succeed academically and be better able to resist negative peer pressure. We, too, support these ideas. Yet, we in no way intend for children to become their own gods or deny the existence of God. The values listed in the curriculum clearly reveal that we intend to help children become compassionate and caring and demonstrate a humble, giving attitude through service and commitment to others.

Issue 8—Decision-Making/Non-Directive Education:

Response • Dr. Stephen Glenn (1986) wrote in *Raising Children for Success* that children who have a sense of control over their lives believe that "What happens to me is largely a result of the decisions I make and the effort I put forth." Children who do not have this sense of control tend to believe their lives are controlled by others. They may be more vulnerable to negative peer pressure because they don't realize they can make their own decisions and say "no" to harmful activities. We can help children develop this sense of control by allowing them to make decisions at an early age. Children who are never given choices never learn to decide. However, children's decisions need to be guided by adults—at home and at school—who provide appropriate and safe choices.

Issue 9—Hatch Amendment:

Response • We agree with and support the Protection of Pupil Rights Amendment, also referred to as the Hatch Amendment. Parents have a responsibility to be included in their children's education. *PUMSY* is not experimental, nor does it include psychological/psychiatric testing; therefore, it does not violate the Hatch Amendment.

Issue 10—Secular Humanism:

Response • A precise, succinct definition of "secular humanism" is difficult to find. Secular humanism seems to be a belief system that denies the existence of God and/or suggests man is above God. *PUMSY* does not support these ideas. This program is used in public, private-Christian, and parochial schools because the materials reflect the basic values schools and families in our society want communicated to children.

Issue 11—Hypnosis:

Response • The use of relaxation activities with children has been confused with hypnosis because that also requires relaxation. Research information on relaxation makes the point that skill at relaxation improves performance of students in such areas as: learning, test taking, social interaction-skills, self confidence, self-management, lengthened attention span, and higher-order thinking.

Issue 12—"I Am Me, I Am Enough"

Response • Some have interpreted this poster to mean "I Am Enough Without God." That is not the meaning at all. The poster means "I Am Enough Without Drugs, Without Being Rich, Without Being Beautiful. . . ." The poster helps children to counteract beliefs that can interfere with positive self-esteem, such as "I am not pretty enough," "I am not good enough," "I am not smart enough," and so forth. Children cannot think these thoughts and at the same moment feel good about themselves. In the case of this poster, *PUMSY* helps children realize that they are enough, They are good enough; they are pretty enough; they are smart enough. They don't have to do more or perform more or have more to be the valuable, special, lovable people they really are. Children are enough—just the way they are. Being able to say, "I Am Enough" is a key to self-acceptance and is at the core of a positive self image.

Note: *The 1992-updated version has changed "I am Me, I Am Enough" to "I Am Me and I Am OK" to clarify the intent of the author, Jill Anderson.*

The above "Responses to Typical Concerns of Challengers" is from "Report to the Board of Education on *PUMSY: In Pursuit of Excellence*"—Westchester Public School District 92.5, Westchester, Illinois—Sanders (1991) with permission.

Summary

This chapter has covered what to do during a challenge. A general overview by ASCA was provided, followed by more detailed, four-level response by the National School Boards Association. "Strategies for Dealing with Tactics of Censorship Groups" gave nine suggested responses. A copy of a letter being used to "stretch" the intent of the Hatch Amendment was printed in its entirety along with a sample response letter. The chapter concluded with twelve typical challenger concerns with an explanation/response for each.

Chapter 6

Developing and Utilizing Community Support

- Action Flow Chart
- Three Tools for Gaining Support
  Letter Writing
  Information Packets for Key Community Groups
  Presentation to School Board and/or Curriculum Review Committee
- Involving the Media
  Educating Your Community about Censorship
  Tips for Working with the Media
  How to Have a Successful Interview
- Parent Networks
- A Petition Drive
- Other Key Groups to Contact for Support

Greg Brigman and Peggy Moore

Chapter 6

Developing and Utilizing Community Support

In order for any school program including school counseling to be successful, community awareness and support are essential.

The most effective way to gain community support is by having an effective program and letting people know about it. Conducting needs assessments, designing programs to meet needs based on sound educational and counseling principles, evaluating the effectiveness of programs, and communicating with your publics are all part of proven strategies for gaining support.

Regarding challenges to school counseling programs, it is critical for two things to occur: (1) decision makers and the community are aware of the level of support, including local support, for school counseling programs; and (2) decision makers and the community are aware of the issues involving censorship and the educational agenda behind the challenge. The following sections clarify vehicles for accomplishing these two goals.

Action Flow Chart for Developing and Utilizing Community Support

Three levels of challenge and action steps for each level are presented below.

Minor challenges

Challenges are confined to local school(s). There is no media involvement, no flyers sent by challengers to the community, no school board meeting presentations, no phone chain calls to school board members, no public meeting to encourage more challenges. At this level of challenge community involvement includes a local curriculum review committee, a local counseling advisory committee, and PTA officers.

Action Steps

1. Notify principal and district counseling supervisor or assistant superintendent in charge of counseling. Clarify district policy. Having a clear curriculum review policy and following it is the best way to ensure fair evaluation of materials and protect the freedom to learn.

2. Notify other counselors and principals in district of challenge and be sure they know and follow district policy. A letter from a district level administrator would be helpful in encouraging principals to follow district policy.

3. Respond courteously and professionally to parents bringing a challenge and direct them to district policy for challenging materials.

4. Do not allow parents to remove materials from the school for review. Refer them to the district office where one set can be made available. This will ensure that your on-going program is not interrupted during the curriculum review process.

5. If parents would like to observe you while leading a class session, ask them to make an appointment. Since several parents observing at the same time could be disruptive to the lesson and distracting to the children, it is recommended to schedule only one parent per lesson.

6. Meet with your local counseling advisory committee (teachers, parents), your local curriculum review committee, and PTA officers to: (1) make them aware of challenge, (2) provide information about materials being challenged such as why selected, how used, support for use of the program or this type of program (research, guidelines, standards, etc.), and (3) answer questions. This work is critical because it lays a foundation of understanding with key parents and teachers who can be called on to help if the challenge escalates.

Moderate challenges

Materials challenges move beyond local school. One or a few, but not all of the following occur: (1) media reports challengers' concerns, (2) flyers or newsletters are distributed attacking use of materials, (3) school board members receive chain phone calls requesting removal of materials, (4) public meetings are held with the goal of removal of materials, and (5) a group of concerned citizens presents complaints and demands at school board meeting.

Action steps

1. Complete steps 1 to 6 under minor challenges.
2. Curriculum review process is completed at local school(s) and recommendations are provided to district review committee.
3. Contact ASCA and possibly other national organizations for assistance.
4. Counselors meet with supporters of counseling program at the district office level to plan action for addressing challenge. Have a plan to share with them. Being active in giving your side of this issue and following sound policy for reviewing challenges are keys. Delaying getting accurate information out to the community about the program under fire creates more problems and lengthens the challenge process.
5. Have local school principals send information letters to parents and teachers. (See sample on pp. 114-115.)
6. Ask to meet with all principals and counselors (at the level of the challenge, i.e., elementary, middle) and present information packet "A." (See sample presentation outline pp. 117-123.) Ask principals for letter to send their local parents as well as a letter of support signed by all principals.
7. Also, present information packet "A" (see "Information Packets" in this chapter) to: (1) School Board Curriculum Committee; and (2) Local PTA officers, local advisory committee, curriculum review committee, and faculty at local schools.
8. Encourage your superintendent to get a legal opinion from the district's attorney. Provide the attorney with legal background information. (See Chapter 1, Chapter 5, Chapter 8, and Appendix C.)
9. Inform interested parents about parent networks and organizations that fight censorship and strategies they can use to educate the community. (See "Parent Networks" in this chapter.)
10. Meet with local media (newspapers, T.V., radio) to share information from "Presentation to School Board and/or Curriculum Review Committee" (in this chapter) and from packet "A." Also see "Involving Media" in this chapter.

Major challenges

Most or all of the activities listed under moderate challenges occur in addition to some or all of the following: (1) "Stars" of the National Far Right organizations appear at community meetings, (2) board meetings become more hostile as challengers increase level of confrontation, (3) newspaper and T.V. coverage increases, and (4) threatening phone calls are received by board members, review committee members, counselors, and administrators.

1. Complete Action Steps under minor and moderate challenges.

2. Present information packet "B" (see "Information Packets" in this chapter) to: (1) school board, (2) district curriculum review committee (also see "Presentation to school board and/or Curriculum Review Committee" in this chapter), and (3) media.

3. Encourage media to clarify educational agenda of national groups behind challenge as well as the national and local organizations that support school counseling and the research support for the program or type of program under fire. (See "Involving Media" in this chapter.)

4. Increase efforts to encourage parents and other key groups to make their support and opinions known through letters, petitions, phone calls, newsletters, and attendance at board meetings.

5. Make sure you have a support group of friends and colleagues for encouragement during this process. A major challenge is a long and wearing experience. It is important to remind yourself and others of the depth and breadth of support nationally and locally for the important work you are doing. You are not alone in this fight to protect children's access to developmental counseling information and skill training. National, state, and local organizations can provide the supportive help you need. Reach out for this help. (See Chapter 7 for national organizations.)

Three Tools for Gaining Support

The following three tools: (1) letters to newspapers, school board, and parents, (2) information packets for key community groups, and (3) a presentation outline for school board and/or review committee can provide your community with the necessary background to evaluate challenged school counseling materials.

Letter Writing

Writing letters can help inform and educate the community and influence decision makers. Censorship battles can involve many issues, facts, and interpretations. Before you write, give some thought to potential audiences: editors of local newspapers, school board members, school personnel, librarians, book store owners, and local and state elected officials. Then decide what information about the censorship challenge is most pertinent to that particular audience, and which issues and events should be the focus of your letter. Don't cover every detail, but tailor your letter to the intended reader.

Here are some tips for writing an effective letters:

- Keep it short, (no more than two pages—one page is best) and have it typed, if possible.

- Be accurate. Make sure you have the correct name, title, and address of the recipient of your letter. And make sure you present the facts accurately.

- Use your own words to express your personal perspective as a parent, teacher, or student.

- Adopt a constructive tone; don't sound accusatory or threatening.

- Limit the letter to a few carefully worded points. Describe them clearly and back them up with facts.

- State the goal and the action needed to reach that goal. Be sure that the action you request is one that falls within the responsibilities of your reader.

- Remember to commend and thank those working against censorship, as well as to express concern and to request action.

- Sign the letter as an individual unless you have permission to use a group name and are a designated representative of that group.

- Include your address and, when writing to a newspaper, your daytime telephone number.

Samples of letters to newspapers, school board and parents follow.

Sample Parent Letters to Newspapers
by William D. Herlong (with permission)
Sunday, January 24, 1993 Greenville News

I am deeply concerned about the public schools of Greenville County. I believe that the children of our community are entitled to a public education that is well-balanced, thorough, and forward-looking. That right is in danger. A highly-vocal and well-organized pressure group with a potentially destructive agenda may have obtained excessive influence on the Greenville County School Board. In the wake of the November 3rd elections, it was revealed that the group, ironically known as the "Coalition for Excellence in Education" (CEE), endorsed and supported the three new board members. By any measure, the CEE's influence on the 12-member school board is far out of proportion.

If these board members follow the negative agenda of the CEE, as I and many others fear they may, and if the other board members are not solidly unified against that negative agenda, the quality of the public education available in Greenville will be substantially eroded. All of Greenville will suffer if that occurs.

Who is the CEE? What is its agenda? The CEE wants to ban certain books and teaching programs that develop children's abilities to question, reason, and imagine. It claims that such books and programs are actually teaching so-called "New Age" beliefs to children. Its members believe, apparently seriously, that there is a conspiracy to create a "spiritual global consciousness," "one-world socialism," "one-world government and law," and "one-world religion." They claim that "tens of thousands of classroom teachers" are part of this alleged conspiracy.

Members of the local CEE deny that their group is connected to the national CEE (Citizens for Excellence in Education), a group based in California whose stated mission is to "take complete control of all local school boards." However, the local CEE's agenda mirrors that of the national CEE and the more than 900 other local CEE groups around the country. Moreover, the local CEE's information and literature (including the organizing manual "How to Elect Christians to Public Office") come largely from the national CEE.

The founder of the national CEE, the Rev. Robert Simonds, actually advises local CEEs to disavow any connection to him and the national CEE for political reasons. It is easy to see why. Rev. Simonds openly rejects our constitutional separation of church and state. He believes that public school teachers "should be the

Greg Brigman and Peggy Moore

presenters of God's truth" and that children should learn that the world was created "6,000 years ago."

The local CEE wants to suppress the D.A.R.E., S.E.E.D.S., and Tactics for Thinking programs. Parents already have the right to remove their children from programs they object to. The local CEE doesn't want these programs available for any children.

D.A.R.E. is a self-esteem program in which specially trained officers from the Sheriff's Department teach students about substance abuse, how to say "no" to drugs and alcohol, and about physical abuse. Apparently, the local CEE objects to students being taught that they themselves can and must make the decision to say "no." In S.E.E.D.S., volunteer parents read books such as "Peter Rabbit," "Charlotte's Web," and "Sylvester and the Magic Pebble," to students in the third grade and below. Tactics for Thinking attempts to teach students thinking skills that successful students have always learned, either on their own or from good teachers. Before writing about snow, for example, students might be told to imagine themselves as snowflakes falling from the sky.

Nationally, the CEE hasn't stopped with the above programs. For example, in Colorado, CEE members recently attacked Shakespeare's "MacBeth" for emphasizing "death, suicide, ghosts, and Satan." In Texas, they challenged "Little Red Riding Hood" because the grandmother drinks wine. In Ohio, the children's classic "A Wrinkle in Time" was alleged to have "cult implications," "Satanism suggestion," and "indoctrination of the Occult."

It is difficult to see why the local and national CEEs oppose such programs and books. The books are unquestionably valuable and numerous studies have shown that critical thinking and self-esteem programs improve academic achievement, help children think more rationally, and help children resist drugs and teen-age sex.

I believe the CEEs oppose them because they are effective. CEE members do not want children to be taught to ask questions and to think for themselves. They fear children will then question their parents, their church, even the Bible itself. They fear children, when faced with moral challenges, will make the wrong decision.

But we cannot shield our children forever from drugs, sex, alcohol, or even bad words. As Atticus tells his son in "To Kill a Mockingbird," "There's a lot of ugly things in this world, Jem. I wish I could keep them all away from you. But that's never possible." Our children will face unpleasant realities, and they will make their own choices. What we can do is raise them in a loving, moral environment, teaching them by our words and our lives how we believe they should live. In addition, we can ensure that they receive the best education we can manage, one that teaches them not only the "3Rs" but also about life and living in a diverse, complex, and often contentious world. I hope and pray that my four children will make the right choices. But, whether I like it or not, it is they who must choose.

That is why we must not allow the CEE to strip our public schools of the books and programs that encourage real thought and questioning and which build self-confidence and a sense of self-worth. Those are the very books and programs that promote integrity, good character, high morals, and respect for others.

The local CEE has some positive objectives which I share. For example, it apparently supports raising teachers' salaries to levels equal to surrounding counties. Further, the activism of the local members of the CEE is commendable. In a democratic society, we all have the right and responsibility to debate public policy issues. Local CEE members certainly have the right to band together as a political force endorsing and supporting candidates for the school board.

Those of us who do not support their agenda have the same rights. We must exercise them! We must work to ensure that the public schools are allowed to teach children to think rationally and deeply and help develop their self-confidence and self-esteem. We must demand that programs and books be evaluated based on merit (if they have value, use them; if no, don't), and that no particular groups be allowed a veto. We must guard against extremism from either the right or the left and the imposition of any particular group's ideology. Finally, we must vigilantly support our teachers so that they will not be afraid to use approved books and programs even though pressure groups such as the CEE might object.

Above all, we must put aside our apathy and educate ourselves. We cannot depend on "the other guy" to see that our children have access to a quality public education. If we, the concerned citizens and parents of Greenville County, do these things, our public schools will be among the finest in the nation. If we do these things, our community will continue to grow and prosper.

William D. Herlong is a Greenville attorney, active parent at Augusta Circle Elementary School, and a founder of the new citizens group, VOICE, Voters Organized to Improve Children's Education. The concerns of VOICE are the point of Herlong's article.

Sample Letter of Support to School Board

Mrs. Janice Jones, President
Valley District School Board
123 Main Street
Anytown, USA

Dear Ms. Jones:

As a parent of three children in Valley District schools, I am writing to express my concern about the attack on several books being used in the high school. I understand that the critics have claimed that these books "undermine traditional values," and that the books have been removed while a review is being conducted.

I am disturbed by the controversy, because I do not want a small group of people deciding what my children should and should not learn in school. I believe that the removal of these books, even briefly, constitutes an act of censorship, and I ask that the books be replaced as soon as possible. It is my hope that the review process will give the books a fair assessment, according to their educational merit, and restore them to the curriculum.

We should not teach our children to be afraid of controversy. Rather, we should show them clearly that there are democratic ways to resolve such differences. I hope that the Valley District school board will do so by restoring the controversial books and seeing that the review process is thorough and timely.

Sincerely,

Jane Doe
17 Milford Street
Anytown, USA

Sample Letter to a School Board

Dear _____

As a counselor educator at Clemson University who specializes in elementary school counseling and as a concerned community member and parent, I am writing to voice my strong support for the educational programs currently being challenged. It is my opinion that _____ County School District is on very solid footing in promoting the use of these programs.

The programs of concern include your outstanding elementary counseling program and programs used by regular classroom teachers, special education teachers, and counselors that focus on self-esteem, affective education, drug abuse prevention, problem solving and decision making, guided imagery and cooperative learning.

As a former teacher and school counselor and as an educational researcher and university professor, I am familiar with both the practical use of these programs with children and the research base supporting their use.

The research evidence is quite clear that the programs listed above are very helpful in preventing school failure, reducing school dropouts, and helping children learn the skills, attitudes, and knowledge necessary to be successful in school.

I believe the people protesting these programs are acting on the basis of misinformation.

It is my belief that these programs are not religious in nature, are not "New Age" oriented, and are not undermining family or traditional values.

I do believe that these programs are: main stream, based on sound educational principals and research based theory, and are supported by many respected state and national organizations.

Some of the organization which publicly support comprehensive, developmental counseling programs, and the use of the programs listed above include:

- *The National Parent Teacher Association*
- *The American School Counselor Association*
- *Lions Club International*
- *The National School Boards Association*
- *The American Counseling Association*
- *The National Dropout Prevention Center*
- *The South Carolina School Counselor Association*
- *The National Conference of State Legislatures*
- *The South Carolina Association of Counseling and Development*
- *The National Association of Elementary Principals*
- *The College Entrance Exam Board*
- *The National Education Association*

As you can see, the school district is in good company.

Your decision on this matter will have far reaching implications beyond the school counseling program. Teachers K-12 involved in Language Arts, Social Studies, Health, and Home Economics all have specific learning objectives related to at least one of the programs being criticized.

I appreciated the educational leadership you and the rest of the Board of Education has shown by supporting these important programs.

If I can be of help to you in establishing the support for these programs, please feel free to call on me.

Sincerely

Greg A. Brigman, Ph.D.

Sample Letter from a Principal
to Parents and Teachers

Dear Parent,

I am writing to clarify some information you may have received about our school counseling program. The counseling program at Smith Elementary is based on the developmental needs of children and focuses on the skills and attitude needed for school success and healthy development. Our counselor, Mrs. Jones, provides services for all children through classroom guidance lessons and offers small group and individual counseling as needed and requested. Ms. Jones also consults with our teachers and provides services to our parents such as parent conferences, parent education seminars, a parenting resource library, and information on community referral resources.

Our school counseling program is patterned after the most effective school counseling programs in the nation, and is designed to comply with school accrediting standards and state guidelines. Our materials and services reflect the most up-to-date research on helping young people develop the skills they need for effective living and learning.

Recently, some flyers have been circulated in our community questioning some of our school counseling materials. The materials being questioned are _____ which are part of our classroom guidance program for third grade. The school district has a policy in place to insure a fair evaluation of questioned materials. We are following that policy which calls for a written complaint followed by a review of the materials and complaint by a local curriculum review committee. This committee is made up of school personnel, parents, and community leaders. After reviewing the materials and complaint, the committee recommends either to keep or remove the materials. If the recommendation is not satisfactory to the parent bringing the complaint, them the parent can appeal to the district's curriculum review committee (made up of school personnel, parents, and community leaders). If the parent is not satisfied with the recommendation of the district committee, then the parent can appeal directly to the school board.

Greg Brigman and Peggy Moore

We welcome evaluation of any of our curriculum and materials including our school counseling materials. We are proud of our teachers, counselors, and our programs and materials and invite parents to observe our teachers and counselors in the classroom. Any of our materials are available for review at the district office. To help parents to be informed about our school counseling program, Ms. Jones sends several counseling newsletters out each year, has a corner in our school newspaper, gives a presentation on her program at the first PTA meeting each year, has brochures for parents describing her services, and sends home information letters regarding classroom guidance lessons. We believe that the more parents know about our school counseling program, the more supportive they are. Parents, teachers, and students who have had contact with our school counseling programs consistently report very favorable opinions on surveys about the quality of the services.

If you are interested in reviewing (challenged materials), they are available at our district office (address and phone number). If you would like to request a review of any material by our curriculum review committee, please contact our media specialist (name and phone number) or myself. If you would like to observe a classroom guidance lesson or regular teacher lesson, please contact the counselor or teacher to schedule a time.

We appreciate your support and involvement.

Sincerely

Name (Principal)

Information Packets
for Key Community Groups

Parts or all of the following can be shared with key groups at the minor, moderate, and major challenge stages. It is recommended that the packets be presented and summarized in person. The information packets you choose to present should include enough information for decision makers and potential supporters to be able to respond to challenges in a informed manner. The reason for having two packets is to avoid overloading your audience with too much information at one time.

Information Packet "A"

1. Letter to local school parents from principal giving background information on counseling program and specific information about challenged materials. (See this chapter for sample letter.)
2. Brochure describing the school counseling program.
3. Local and state education goals and objectives pertinent to counseling goals and objectives.
4. Regional accrediting standards related to school counseling.
5. National, state, and local organizations that support developmental school counseling. (See Chapter 1.)
6. District policy for reviewing a request to remove curriculum materials.
7. Brochure (if available) or overview of challenged program.
8. Two articles from National PTA: *The National PTA's Guide to Extremism* and Fege (1991) *Censorship in the Schools: Parents Can Protect the Freedom to Learn.*
9. Two articles from National School Boards Association, Morris (1992) and Jones (1993), gave excellent overviews of the censorship movement and practical steps to take when censorship challenges arise. The Morris article appears in Chapter 5. Chapter 7 gives a list of key articles and resources.

Information Packet "B"

1. Parts or all of Chapters 1, 2, 3, and 8 of this book

2. *Children Achieving Potential,* (Glossoff & Koprowicz, 1990), gave an excellent overview and rationale for developmental counseling as well as supporting research.

3. *Comprehensive School Counseling Programs: A Review for Policy Makers,* (Borders, & Drury, 1992), offered an extensive review of 30 years of research which provided strong evidence of effectiveness of various school counseling services, including classroom guidance and small group counseling.

For more information on the use of Packets "A" and "B," see the Chapter 5 section titled "Strategies for Dealing with Tactics of Censorship Groups."

Presentation to School Board and/or Curriculum Review Committee

When your local school board begins to receive phone calls from concerned citizens and hears accusations at board meetings, it is natural for their level of concern to be raised toward your program/materials. You can be very helpful to them, if after reviewing the goals and objectives of your guidance and counseling program, you make a presentation which encompasses the following components:

1. **Definitions:** Give a definition of comprehensive developmental guidance and counseling. This definition should include the basic principles of a developmental counseling program, and the comprehensive range of activities and services that it provides. Two examples of definitions are given below:

   a. The following definition of developmental guidance is from The American School Counselor Association (1990).

   The American School Counselor Association recognizes and supports the implementation of comprehensive developmental counseling programs at all educational levels. The programs are designed to help all students develop their educational, social, career, and personal strengths and to become responsible and productive citizens. School counselors help create and organize these programs, as well as provide appropriate counselor interventions.

School counseling programs are developmental by design, focusing on needs, interests, and issues related to the various stages of student growth. There are objectives, activities, special services and expected outcomes, with an emphasis on helping students to learn more effectively and efficiently. There is a commitment to individual uniqueness and the maximum development of human potential. A counseling program is an integral part of a school's total educational program.

b. Robert Myrick is a nationally recognized leader in developmental school counseling and a professor in the Department of Counselor Education, College of Education at the University of Florida. In his widely used textbook, *Developmental Guidance and Counseling* (1987, 1993) he defined the developmental approach as follows:

> *"The developmental approach is an attempt to identify certain skills and experiences that students need to have as part of their going to school and being successful. Learning behaviors and tasks are identified and clarified for students. Then, a guidance curriculum is planned which complements the academic curriculum. In addition, life skills are identified and these are emphasized as part of preparing students for adulthood."*

Myrick also stated that the *basic principles* of a developmental counseling program are:

> *"It is for all students;*
>
> *It has an organized and planned curriculum;*
>
> *It is sequential and flexible;*
>
> *It is an integral part of the total educational process;*
>
> *It involves all school personnel;*
>
> *It helps students learn more effectively and efficiently; and*
>
> *It includes counselors who provide specialized counseling services and interventions."*

The school counseling program is comprehensive in the *range of activities* and services that it provides:

> *Preventive classroom guidance activities;*
>
> *Individual and group counseling;*

Referrals to community agencies;

Consultation with teachers, administrators, parents, and community leaders;

Crisis intervention; and

Assessment, placement, and follow-up services.

2. **District Goals**: Give your district's guidance goals and objectives and clarify how these goals promote the district's general educational goals.

3. **State Goals**: Give your state guidance goals and objectives and/ or your state's general educational goals and objectives which will more than likely reflect language suggesting education of the whole child (academic, affective, and physical). Because the educational paradigm is moving to educating the whole child, it is important that school counseling programs are comprehensive and developmental.

4. **Accrediting Standards**: Most schools choose to follow regional accrediting standards. For example, one such accrediting body is the Southern Association of Colleges and Schools. Under Student Services and Activities, which includes Guidance, the following standards are stated:

   1. *The school shall provide comprehensive guidance services for all students. Guidance counselors, administrators, and teachers shall share the responsibilities for providing those services.*

   2. *The guidance program shall be developmental in nature and provide for individual and group counseling, group guidance, and staff development activities to assist teachers in understanding the nature of the student at various stages of development.*

   (Pointing out how your program meets these requirements can be one important answer to the question, "Why do we go into the classrooms, offer small groups, etc.?")

5. **National Guidelines**: Nationally, a very important report was released in 1991 by the United States Department of Labor. *The Secretary's Commission on Achieving Necessary Skills (SCANS) Report for America 2000* gave a three-part foundation of skills and qualities that will be essential preparation for all students, both those going directly to the work place and those planning further education. (Part I—Basic Skills: reading, writing, arithmetic/ mathematics, listening, speaking; Part 2—Thinking Skills: cre-

ative thinking, decision making, seeing things in the mind's eye, problem solving, knowing how to learn, and reasoning; Part 3— Personal Qualities: responsibility, self-esteem, sociability, self-management, and integrity/honesty.

The National Association for the Education of Young Children (NAEYC) developed a position statement on *Developmentally Appropriate Practice in Early Childhood Programs Serving Children* from birth through age eight. NAEYC believes that a high quality program provides a safe and nurturing environment that promotes the social, emotional, cognitive, and physical development of young children (Hohenshil & Brown, 1991).

The National Association of Elementary School Principals (NAESP) published a set of program standards titled *Early Childhood Education and the Elementary School Principal: Standards for Quality Programs for Young Children.* The list of quality indexes that are important to school counselors are:

1. Helping develop a positive self-image;
2. Enhancing social and emotional development;
3. Encouraging independent thinking and developing problem-solving skills;
4. Improving communication skills.

These three sources give clear implications for school curricula selection for the education of the whole child. The guidance goals and objectives of your district/school should blend very effectively with your state and regional goals and objectives, which blend directly with national goals and objectives. Use this information to confirm the foundation for your comprehensive developmental guidance and counseling program/model.

6. **Rationale:** In addition to numbers 1 through 5, an excellent rationale for a comprehensive developmental guidance and counseling program/model can be found in *Children Achieving Potential* (Glosoff & Koprowicz, 1990). This document was produced jointly by the National Conference of State Legislatures and the American Association for Counseling and Development. It is singularly one of the best documents available for rationale, research, and state-by-state policies regarding elementary school counseling. Information for ordering is available in Chapter 7.

7. **Statistics**: In addition to the general rationale above, you should include your state and local statistics in the areas of dropout rates, grade-level failures, pregnancy rates, alcohol and drug use at various levels, child abuse numbers, and so forth. These statistics have tremendous implications for the use of materials that promote self-esteem, problem-solving and decision-making skills, learning skills and social skills. These skills and how students feel about themselves have an impact on their academic performance. (See Chapter 2—Research.) National statistics are easily obtainable from various agencies with which you work.

8. **Selection criteria**: You should include the criteria you use to select materials. The guidelines for selection could include the following questions:

   A. Are the learning objectives and focus of the program compatible with the school district's educational goals?

   B. Are the materials age appropriate for the students involved?

   C. Is there support in the research literature for the type of program being evaluated?

   D. Is this program based on widely accepted educational techniques?

   E. Is there ongoing input from parents, teachers, and students?

   It is important to check to see if your state/district has definite guidelines for the selection of curricula. If so, these guidelines should be included in your rationale.

9. **Research**: A review of the research literature related to comprehensive developmental guidance and counseling programs and the types of materials used to meet your goals and objectives is very supportive. The following areas have empirical data supporting their use, and the documentation for this research can be found in Chapter 2—Research:

   1. Developmental Counseling

   2. Self-Esteem

   3. Affective Education

   4. Relaxation and Imagery

   5. Thinking Skills and Cooperative Learning

   Also, see Borders and Drury (1992) and Glosoff and Koprowcz, 1990).

10. **Parents Concerns:** You may choose to address parental concerns in your report. A comprehensive list, though not inclusive, has been provided in Chapter 5. These can be used as samples for your consideration.

    You may also choose to give examples of how some of the techniques that are the source of the concerns are very useful in the educational setting, are not harmful, and in fact have long histories as proven teaching/educational techniques (i.e., guided imagery, relaxation).

11. **Psychological Opinion:** It may or may not be necessary for you to have statements regarding a psychological opinion.

12. **Legal Opinion:** Legal opinions as to violations of the Hatch Amendment (Protection of Pupil Rights), First and Fourteenth Amendments are valuable and can be obtained from your district's attorney. Other legal information is found in Chapters 1, 5, 8, and Appendix C.

13. **Support From Key Groups:** Support from key groups of parents, teachers, businesses, administrators, churches, educational organizations, governmental agencies, and so forth is vital. Support can come in the way of letters to the Superintendent, letters to the editor of local newspapers, radio talk shows, speakers in support at board meetings, calls from supportive citizens to counselors and administrators, and so forth. It is extremely important for you to keep your peers and supervisors advised of the same information you have regarding a challenge. If they have the correct information, they will be your greatest advocates. They, in turn, will be able to respond in their communities, churches, families, and so forth. Meeting with local community organizations is very helpful because most of them have only heard pieces of any controversy. You will be able to give them correct information and be available to answer any questions they may have. It is at this time that brochures on the program/materials attacked could be made available along with selected or all areas of this presentation. Two examples of community support in the form of a letter to the editor and a parent newsletter are in this chapter.

14. **Conclusion:** Give short summary statements on: (1) the local guidance goals and objectives as they relate to state, regional, and national educational goals for all students; (2) the rationale for selecting a comprehensive developmental guidance and counseling program/model; and (3) the selection criteria for the specific material being challenged. Then give conclusions drawn from the empirical data that supports the program or type of program(s)

used to implement your goals and objectives. The total conclusion or summary should be very concise. The total presentation could take approximately thirty minutes in time. The printed presentation could range from 10 to 50 plus pages. Presenting the printed material with a professional cover, table of contents, list of review committee members and positions (if applicable), numbered pages, double spaced (where appropriate) makes your document "user friendly" for the school board or review committee. A professional presentation will confirm the excellent program that you are providing for your district/school.

Involving the Media

Educating Your Community About Censorship and Academic Freedom

One powerful way to gain community support is to involve the media in clarifying the nature of censorship as endangering the rights of citizens, in particular, academic freedom. Some ideas are listed below to help bring this issue of academic freedom to light. This information is from the National Council for Self-Esteem.

- **Your community wants to know when their rights as citizens are endangered.** This may be one of those times. The media can be of tremendous help in conveying these concerns about academic freedom.

- **Be proactive** in dealing with the media. They understand and can appreciate concerns about academic freedom.

- **Locate knowledgeable spokespersons** to explain concerns about the potential loss of academic freedom.

- **Share information you have received from organizations** helping you protect academic freedom in your community. It is helpful for the community to know about the educational agenda of the groups behind most challenges.

- **Be prepared to share a list of people the media may wish to interview.** The list might include:
  a. Concerned parents who support academic freedom.
  b. Parents who can attest to the tangible value of guidance programs and also the specific materials under discussion.
  c. Local supportive ministers.

    d. Teachers who have seen improvements in their classroom environment as a result of the guidance program(s) under discussion.

    e. Contact persons from national organizations. They can provide background information. Also, they can help the media see the overall picture of how your local situation may tie into a national trend of increased censorship of educational programs covering a broad range of topics, including sex education, drug education, guidance, and reading programs.

- Remain focused on the basic issue: Children in your school district are at risk of losing their academic freedom.

Tips for Working with the Media

Good press coverage of your efforts to stop censorship in your community can be a valuable asset. Favorable media attention can help influence decision-makers and alert supporters you didn't know you had. It can also help create a climate for a satisfactory conclusion to the problem.

Don't be intimidated by the media. They are made up of people whose job it is to find and sell news to your community. Often, they are overworked, which means they may be too busy to seek out a story like yours. But with good preparation, you can make their job easier—and get your story before the public—by bringing your issue to their attention clearly and concisely. An unfolding censorship story is one likely to affect and interest most of your community, so approach the media with confidence. (See "Sample Parent Letter to Newspaper" in this chapter.)

Following are some tips to help you get media coverage for your efforts to protect your children's education.

Contacting the Press:

- Develop an accurate and comprehensive list of media people. Include city editors at daily and weekly area newspapers, assignment editors at local radio and television stations, and the statewide Associated Press. Call to get their names and the names and titles of the reporters who cover education issues.

Mail addressed to Ms. Betty Smith, City Editor, is more likely to be opened promptly than that addressed to the City Editor.

- Learn to write crisp, clear news releases. News releases are used to announce important meetings or decisions, to publicize events, or to make statements. A news release should be no longer than two pages, typed, double-spaced, and include the name and telephone number of a spokesperson to call with questions. The first paragraph should always include who, what, where, when and why. Your group's point of view should be expressed in quotations from your spokesperson. Mail news releases to your media list, then be sure a member of your group is prepared to answer questions and provide further information.

- Call your media contacts regularly to be assured of successful news coverage. Use these calls to alert the media to fast-breaking news, to follow up on your news release, to remind them of an important meeting or decision, or to let reporters who missed an important meeting know what occurred. Have the pertinent information in front of you when you make these calls so that you can be succinct and accurate.

What to Say:

There are certain points that need to be made regarding nearly every attack on the freedom to learn. Repeat these over and over again—especially to reporters. Here are a few points to commit to memory; modify them to suit your situation:

- "Those people trying to (choose one: remove books from our classrooms/rewrite history/teach religion in science classes/eliminate sex education from our schools) have every right to voice their opinions, and we welcome their doing so. Parental and community involvement is an important part of public education. But, let's not confuse local control with vocal control. We don't want a small minority—no matter how loud—dictating what all of our children learn or don't learn."

- "This is not an isolated incident happening here in (name of community). It's part of a national anti-public-education movement that involves groups like Eagle Forum, Concerned Women for America, and Citizens for Excellence in Education. These groups want public schools to teach their own particular sectarian point of view. I'd be glad to show you their literature and give you information about where and when it has been distributed before."

- "While we're all concerned about this (choose one: book, curriculum, film, program, activity), we must remember that this is not just an issue of censorship. It involves our children's right to learn in public, tax-supported schools. These censorship efforts are really an organized attack on public education, and we are working to protect our public schools."

How to Say It:

How your perspective is described by the media depends on two things—your credibility and your image. Establishing credibility with the media takes time and effort. Here are some suggestions.

- Only call or write to the media when you have news to report—don't pester them with peripheral matters. You want them to know that when you call, it's important.

- Be prepared. Media people work under time and space constraints, so they appreciate timely, reliable, and concise information. Ask if they are "on deadline," so that you will know if you can supply the information in time. Accuracy is especially important. If your media contacts come to see you as a good source of information, they will be more likely to cover your issues and contact you again. Get the information and call back. Giving wrong information to reporters can put a quick end to your relationship with them.

- Be persistent, but not a pest. Don't give up if an editor or reporter doesn't seem interested at first. Keep reminder calls brief, keep trying, and remain friendly.

- Never make a personal attack on the media or those who oppose your point of views. Stick to the issues, facts and principles involved. If an attack is made on your group, don't feel compelled to respond. You don't want a lot of name-calling to obscure the principles you're defending.

Establishing an image takes some thought and planning. Keep the following suggestions in mind.

- Whenever possible, appoint or elect one spokesperson. More than one will confuse the media and the public. Choose someone who is on top of the issues and who is confident in dealing with the media.

- Always make clear whom the spokesperson represents. If you've organized a pro-public-education group that includes a clergy, parents, teachers, community leaders, and others, say so. If you can show the diversity of each group for the broadcast media, do so.

- Be aware of the tone and image created by any written materials or graphics that you produce. Strive for an easy-to-understand presentation that is professional but not slick.

- Remember that you are dealing with two branches of the media—print and broadcast. Television reporters are preoccupied with the visual aspects of a story; they are unlikely to cover something unless it will look interesting on film. Keep this in mind when you choose a location for events and announcements. Don't be afraid to be dramatic and creative in "setting the stage."

- Finally, always keep media coverage in perspective. A good story won't win your battle for you, and a bad one won't lose it.

From *Protecting the Freedom to Learn,* (1989) p. 31-32. People For the American Way, with permission.

How to Have a Successful Interview

- Know in advance the points you want to highlight. Make a list of no more than three points you want to get across, then find a way to fit them into the interview. *If you offer too much information, your interview will be confusing and the reporter won't be able to put together a good story.*

- Never say anything you don't want to see in print or hear on the air. This includes casual remarks, jokes, personal comments, and opinions.

- Answer only what you are asked. Don't elaborate unless the three points you want to make are not covered in the questions.

- Be spontaneous. That leaves a better impression with the public.

- Never say "no comment."

- Don't ask for questions in advance. It's okay to ask for the general areas the reporter will be interested in talking about so you can be better prepared.

- Don't ask to see the story before it runs.

- Understand the requirements of an interview for print, TV, and radio and be prepared to be interviewed for each. If you aren't familiar with the differences, ask local reporters about their expectations.

- Be concise. The jargon that you use internally is not appropriate for the media or any other outside audience. Use language that clearly and simply describes what you are doing.
- Anticipate what will be asked and think through your answers to those questions. Then, you'll always be prepared.

From the Education Commission of the States (ECS), (1991) with permission.

Parent Networks

This section provides information about citizen organizations that help protect student rights against censorship. Ideas for communicating community support are also presented and include: letter writing, petition drive, phone networks, newsletters and board meetings.

Citizen Organizations

Two organizations that help protect the freedom to learn are the National PTA and the Freedom to Learn Network. The National PTA publishes a brochure titled the "National PTA's Guide to Extremism" which covers extremist strategies, extremist beliefs, and how your PTA can combat extremism. Their publication, *PTA Today,* also featured an article by Fege (1991) Censorship in the Schools: Parents can Protect the Freedom to Learn, which conveys the concerns of the National PTA with the censorship movement and offers suggestions for parents interested in protecting the freedom to learn. (See Chapter 7 for address and phone number.)

The Freedom to Learn Network is a citizen's organization created in 1992 to promote educational freedom and expose the motives, it believes, are behind most curriculum challenges. A statement of purpose by the Freedom to Learn Network follows along with their address.

The Freedom to Learn Network

The Freedom to Learn Network was formed early in 1992 in response to widespread attacks against books and programs in local public schools. Citizens for Excellence in Education (CEE), whose goal is the destruction of public education, is attacking drug and alcohol programs, self-esteem programs, and health, sex and AIDS education.

The Freedom to Learn Network does not blanket its endorsement of all programs, but chooses to expose the motives behind these challenges. The Freedom to Learn Network continues to add districts and concerned citizens in the Lehigh Valley, and the state of Pennsylvania, to the organization. While CEE strives to align itself with taxpayer groups and those that can be taken in by their propaganda, the Freedom to Learn Network strives to provide accurate information, not slanted by personal beliefs or agendas.

The Freedom to Learn Network believes that all children, regardless of race or religion, have the basic right to educational freedom.

Freedom to Learn Network
P.O. Box 21352
Lehigh Valley, Pennsylvania 18002-1352
(610) 838-2254

Two other citizen organizations that can help communities protect the freedom to learn are listed below:

The Community Coalition Network
4690 North Lane
De Mar, CA 92014
Contact: Polly Dennis

VOICE—Voters Organized to Improve
Children's Education
PO Box 1125
Greenville, SC 29602-1125
(803) 244-0598

Concerned parents who want to organize local parent support against censorship can benefit from contacting these sources.

Two examples of parent network publications follow.

Examples of Parent Network Publications

Dear Friend of the Schools,

Back in September, you signed a petition stating that, as a voter and taxpayer of _____County, you supported Affective Education. When you signed this petition the third graders' self-esteem program, PUMSY, was under attack. A very vocal minority in our community complained about this curriculum, calling it New Age Religion because of its use of relaxation, guided imagery, and emphasis on self reliance. Unfortunately, this was just the beginning of their fight against this type of teaching in our schools. There were nineteen official complaints lodged against the PUMSY program (out of an elementary school population of approximately 4,000 students), and on several of these complaint forms there were statements calling for a ban on all affective curricula. In case you're confused by the term "affective education," we defined it as anything that addresses the social and emotional development of a student. This is a part of the educationally sound approach of teaching to the "whole" child. Other programs that are considered "affective" are: Quest, Sex Education, Creative Writing, Higher Order Thinking Skills, Whole Language, Conflict Resolution, Creative Movement, and so forth. Already, the people who attacked PUMSY and asked for a ban on affective education have begun specifying some of these other programs as offensive to them. They have proposed school district policy changes that would eliminate any teaching they do not agree with. Some have even begun demanding the removal of books from school library shelves, books they deem unsuitable.

Fortunately, we live in a democracy where this minority has a right to speak its mind. And in our school system, there is a policy that a parent may object to curricula and to books that his or her child is exposed to and that suitable alternatives will be found for the child. However, a parent's rights extend only to his or her own child, not to the rest of the school population. When they try to dictate what books and learning materials are used for the rest of the students—this is censorship.

Several months ago, when this issue of PUMSY first arose, the school board responded to the nineteen complaints by establishing a committee of eighteen to review the PUMSY material, to hear the complainants speak, and to determine if the PUMSY *material was suitable. This eighteen person committee was made up of educators, parents, businessmen, and clergy. In December, the committee voted 15 to 3 to keep the* PUMSY *curriculum in the schools. They presented their report to the school board on December 17. At that time, the school board chose to put off making the final vote until January 19, 1993. For those present at the December 17 meeting, it was apparent that several school board members were hesitant to vote in favor of accepting the committee's recommendation. One school board member admitted that he had been keeping a tally by his phone to determine how many people called urging him to vote in favor of the program versus those who opposed it. Our calls make a difference. That is why we are writing to you today. Enclosed with this letter is a list of the school board members, their addresses and phone numbers. Please, take the time to write a note or call the board members and let them know you support the review committee's recommendation to keep* PUMSY.

Perhaps you feel you do not know enough about the PUMSY *program to voice such support for it. If you do want to study the program, we recommend that you call the guidance counselor of a nearby elementary school and ask to look over the material. On the other hand, you may just want to call the school board members to state your general support of affective education, which includes such programs as* PUMSY. *If we let this extremely conservative religious minority have its way on the issue of* PUMSY, *there's no telling what other educational programs will come under attack next. Please, help us stop this censorship movement in our community. Help us protect our children's freedom to learn. Call or write the school board members before the January 19 deadline. Thank you for your continued support.*

Sincerely,

xxxxxxxxx

VOICE
VOTERS ORGANIZED TO IMPROVE CHILDREN'S EDUCATION

Introduction

Welcome to the second issue of Voice's newsletter. We have much to report.

Operating Budget

The process of establishing the budget for next year is underway. The board has already held several meetings and workshops. To date, no decisions have been made.

The Administration projects a shortfall of $5,707,710 out of a total operating budget of $172,249,924. (It was revealed on Sunday that the shortfall may in fact be $600,000 greater, or $6.3 million.) The Administration recommends increasing taxes by 3.5 mills (the board has authority to increase by up to 4 mills without Legislative approval) to bring in an additional $2,975,000. It recommends salary increases totaling $2,492,000 (bus drivers get 50 cents an hour more; other personnel get a 1.7% increase). After the salary increases the budget then remains $5,224,710 out of balance. To address, the Administration has proposed cuts totaling $5,245,600. The cuts are as follows:

Item	Projected Savings
Implement contract food services program in all schools	360,000
Reducing funding for Governor's School for Arts	50,000
Retain budget caps from 1992-93 budget	225,300
Close one career center	750,000
Waive board policy requiring 1% of revenue to reserve fund	1,700,000
Increase driver's education fee from $25 to $55	40,000
Elim. 4 of the 8 curriculum coordinator positions	1 86,000
Elim. all 31.5 reading teacher positions	1,200,000
Reduce staffing from in-school suspension by half and eliminate fund for supplies	508,000

Greg Brigman and Peggy Moore

Reduce info. services from five to four positions	37,000
Elim. 2 of the 4 community coordinator positions	55,300
Reduce funding for Singing Christmas Tree	2,800
Reduce funding for Roper Mountain Science Center by 10% (probably reduction in staff)	78,000
Elim. District staff meeting	7,400
Elim. the Wellness program	5,000
Reduce by 5% funding for Fine Arts Center (probably reduction in staff)	32,800
Elim. District's Personnel Directory	8,000

The trustees' positions on these reductions are becoming clearer. One faction of the board appears to believe that only classroom teachers are important. Ms. Hershey, for example, has stated: "I don't care for paying for social workers. I don't like psychologists, either." (Psychologists salaries amount to $763,327; social workers are about $300,000. These positions are largely necessary, among other reasons to do the testing required by law. Each of the district's 17 psychologists does more than 250 evaluations per year.) Several trustees appear to believe that funds from the capital budget (see below) can be used in the operating budget. Mr. Dill has complained about the facilities plan, arguing that the money should be used for school maintenance before new schools are built or old schools upgraded. Unfortunately, construction comes from the capital budget and maintenance comes from the operating budget, and the two budgets cannot be commingled.

Several trustees oppose eliminating the reading teacher positions (savings of $1,200,0000—the administration contends they are largely duplicative). Others seem to oppose eliminating a career center (savings of $750,000). On the other hand, Ms. Hershey appears to oppose even the 3.5 mill tax increase. Neither she nor any other trustee has come up with any alternative plan to achieve the savings necessary to balance the district's budget.

The Greenville County Taxpayers Association has a plan, however. Grady Miller has proposed a 25% across the board cut in all administrative expenses. (Note: The district is already about the most efficient in the entire state. The administrative overhead per student is among the lowest of any district in the state). He would have the district cut two of four area offices, have the Greenville Transit Authority take over maintenance of the district's bus fleet, and further trim special programs including the International Baccalaureate program, the Fine Arts Center, and the Roper Mountain Science Center.

There has been no discussion of raising taxes the full 4 mills allowable without legislative approval (an additional $425,000 could be raised that way). Likewise no one has suggested going to the Legislature for an increase greater than 4 mills even though more than 4 mills may be necessary even for conservative funding of school programs—especially if the reading teachers and career center (together equaling cuts of $1.95 million are not eliminated).

Nor has anyone suggested eliminating unnecessary perks for Trustees, (e.g., only the Trustees who are on a given committee should get a free lunch when they attend a lunch meeting of that committee.)

Capital Budget/Facilities Plan

There has been a development in Columbia that seriously impacts the district's facilities plan. Over the past several years with extensive input from the community, the board developed a plan to provide the school facilities necessary if our children are to receive the quality education they deserve. The facilities plan addresses the need to update seriously aging buildings and to rectify the omission of routine maintenance for so many years on so many buildings because of lack of funds. If also addresses current and projected overcrowding in schools and the need to build new schools in certain areas due to population shifts. Over 1800 people from across the county were involved in developing the facilities plan. All told, over $321,000,000 of construction is planned over 14 years.

A key aspect of funding the construction is the conversion of certain 13-year bonds to 5-year bonds. The 5-year bonds carry a lower interest rate. The district would save at least $215,000 in interest right off the top over the first four years. In addition, they rollover much quicker, thereby freeing up debt capacity to fund subsequent school renovation and construction projects.

Senator David Thomas has managed to get included in the Senate Finance Committee's Appropriation Bill a proviso that, if passed, would delay the facilities plan and dramatically increase the cost of the construction.

The Thomas Proviso prevents the district from converting its 13-year bonds to 5-year bonds if the money necessary to pay off the old bonds and service the new ones is more than 5% greater than the money required to service the old ones. If it converts the 13-year bonds to 5-year bonds as contemplated, the school district's monthly payments will be about 9% greater. (In real terms, it is 2.4 mills greater which is less than $7 on a $75,000 house.) Hence, it could not perform the conversion.

The Thomas Proviso would delay the facilities plan, a year or so for the projects near the beginning, 3-4 years for the projects near the end. The delay in construction would mean the construction will cost nearly $19,000,000 more in the end (assuming 2% inflation). It will probably cost more since the delay will mean more work will have to be done to renovate neglected schools. In addition, it prevents the district from saving the $215,000 due to lower interest rates. Of course, it also means our children will be stuck in substandard, over-crowded schools for that much longer.

We have now learned that a compromise has been reached to allow the facilities plan to go forward, at least for now. The 5% limit in the Thomas Proviso has been increased to 12%. The district's plan will be able to go forward. However, it will remain subject to micro-management from Columbia. This provision should not be in the law at all. We are hopeful that it will be removed entirely from the final budget.

Instruction Committee 5/18 Meeting

The instruction committee met numerous teachers and parents at J.L. Mann High School. The teachers discussed the progress the school has made over the last few years since implementing a new schedule which calls for 90 rather than 50 minute periods, allowing more in-depth study and putting more responsibility on students. Teachers have adopted a "student as worker" philosophy. Education is increasingly hands-on, interdisciplinary, and cooperative, and less lecture-based. Mann's test scores have significantly improved; its drop-out rate has decreased; and it has become a model for schools around the state. Nonetheless, Trustee Julie Hershey did not seem to like Mann's approach to teaching. She stated that the businessmen she has spoken to do not have a problem with people's ability to work together and only want people with expertise. (**Note:** CEE literature is highly critical of programs like Mann's.)

Board's 5/13 "Called" Meeting

The board approved a resolution "strenuously oppos[ing]" the Thomas Proviso (see above) and urging all members of the State Legislative Delegation from Greenville to oppose it. The debate was bitter, but the resolution carried. Julie Hershey, Joe Dill, Ann Sutherlin, and Dwight Loftis voted against it.

Board's Regular May Meeting (5/11)

The meeting was notable primarily because of several speakers. An uplifting speech was made by a woman who described herself as a conservative Christian. She and her husband had their children in a private Christian school until seven years ago. They decided at that time to send them to public school. She said there were some adjustments, but that generally the change was very good. Her values had been generally upheld, and she and her husband had been pleased with the experience. They were not interested in having the public school promote their religious views; they wanted their children to be taught to think independently.

A student from Southside High School spoke on the policy adopted by the Board May 4 concerning school prayer at graduation. That policy allows prayer so long as it is requested by the graduating students and is non-sectarian and non-proselytizing. The student suggested that there be a moment of silence instead so each person could pray however he or she wished.

A representative of the Greenville County Taxpayers Association objected to the proposed 3.5 mills tax increase (or any tax increase). He proposed to save money by not having Maya Angelou speak at the Fine Arts Center.

Fundraiser

Our fundraiser at the Cafe and Then Some was a great success. We netted nearly $1,600. We gave the cast a standing ovation, and they applauded us for what we are trying to do for Greenville's schools.

Legislation

The Thomas Proviso in the Senate Finance Committee Appropriations Bill is discussed above.

S.247 (Peeler): Requires one minute of voluntary silent prayer at beginning of each day—passed House, now in Senate Education Subcommittee.

H.3685 (Fair): Requires State Superintendent and Board of Education to integrate traditional concepts into the reform of public schools - referred to committee.

H.3387 (Fair): Mandates one hour per week release time from school for religious instruction—referred to committee.

Legislative information is available by calling (800) 922-1539.

Copies of specific bills and/or "subject reports" (which list legislation relating to specific subjects (e.g., education) is available free of charge.

Bad News

Glenn Stiegman, the assistant superintendent for finance and operations, has resigned and will be taking a position with a district in Spartanburg County. Glenn's experience and ability were outstanding. His departure will be felt acutely.

Miscellaneous

Important phone numbers and addresses

Upcoming Board Meetings:

6/1   Finance Committee (12:15 p.m.)

6/1   Special Called Board Meeting on Budget (6-9 p.m.)

6/7   2nd Special Called Board Meeting on Budget (6-9 p.m.)

6/8   General Board Meeting (7:30 p.m.)

Newsletter

If your name or address is incorrect, please let us know at the above address. If you would like to add others to our mailing list, let us know that too. If you have comments or suggestions or want to help, or for information on VOICE, please call. . . .

VOICE—Voters Organized to Improve Children's Education
PO Box 1125
Greenville, SC 29602-125
(803) 244-0598

A Petition Drive

Petition drives have several advantages. They can be used to educate the community, influence decision-makers, attract other volunteers, and gain the attention of the media. Some disadvantages are that drives can be time consuming, require a large number of volunteers, and drift on to an inconclusive end.

Petition drives work best when carried out in a relatively short period of time and when the results can be presented at a public forum likely to attract the attention of the media (for example, a school board meeting). Before investing time and energy in a petition drive, assess the circumstances in your community. Are they conducive to a successful petition drive?

If you decide to conduct a petition drive, here are some suggestions:

Planning

Determine a deadline for completing your drive, choosing one that involves a public event, if possible, at which you can present your petition. This will also help you decide who the audience is for your petition. If there isn't an important date that you can link to the drive, set a deadline anyway. Activities like this that involve volunteers need to maintain momentum and a sense of urgency. Establish goals for signatures; how many will you need to declare your drive successful? If there is a great deal of interest in the community in the issue, alert the press to your drive or invite them to a "kick-off" meeting when you launch the drive.

The Petition

Keep your petition focused, clear, brief, action-oriented, and aimed at a specific audience. Be sure that your demands fall within the jurisdiction and responsibilities of those to whom you will present the petition. Identify the sponsoring organizations. This may simply be your group, or you may want to enlist the assistance of other local groups as co-sponsors. Include information on where the completed petitions will be sent. Don't threaten, make personal attacks, alienate potential signers, or be strident.

Gathering Signatures

Once you have determined a deadline for your drive and the number of signatures needed for success, estimate the number of volunteers you need to circulate petitions. Try to involve as many people as possible—better to exceed your goal than to fall short. The list of places to gather signatures is endless: churches, shopping malls, supermarkets, movie theaters, factories, office buildings, and apartment complexes. Have volunteers in these locations at the busiest hours—just before and just after work, and at lunchtime.

Don't expect people to read even the shortest message. Start a friendly conversation and explain concisely why you are circulating the petition and what you hope to accomplish. Have a supply of blank petitions available and enlist the help of the most enthusiastic signers by giving them some to circulate.

Presenting the Petition

Use your results to gauge how much attention you want to draw to your work. If the drive went well, achieving or surpassing your goals, try to present your petition publicly and work to get the media to cover it. It's important to draw attention to your success; it keeps people informed about the issue and builds morale for your side. If the drive didn't go as well as hoped, present the petition during office hours.

From the Education Commission of the States (ECS), (1991) with permission.

Other Key Groups to Contact for Support

The following groups typically support public education, have a vested interest in censorship issues and can provide important community support.

1. Bookstore Owners
2. Radio Talk Shows and Local Broadcasters
3. Parent-School Organizations
4. Town and County Librarians/Media Specialists
5. Retired Educators
6. Chamber of Commerce
7. Civic Organizations
8. Artists and Art Associations

Summary of Ideas for Developing and Utilizing Community Support

This chapter has focused on how to make visible to decision makers the community support for your programs that already exists. Another focus was on how to educate your community about the importance and appropriateness of school counseling programs and about the educational agenda behind many of the challenges.

An Action Flow Chart was presented that detailed action steps for three phases on challenges: minor, moderate, and major.

A section on three tools for gaining support highlighted an information letter from the school principal to parents and teachers, a two-stage information packet, and a presentation outline for school boards and curriculum review committees.

Additional sections on involving the media and helping parent networks were offered. The chapter concluded with a list of local groups to contact for support.

Chapter 7

Helpful Organizations and Resources When a Challenge Occurs

- Organizations
- Resources
- Key Articles

  Important Books and Booklets

  Other Important Books

  Helpful Newsletters

  Research and Tips from Publishers

  Staying Up-to-Date

Greg Brigman and Peggy Moore

Chapter 7

Helpful Organizations and Resources When a Challenge Occurs

There are many organizations and resources available to help school counselors when a challenge to their program occurs.

Organizations

Two keys to receiving the most help from any of the following groups are: (1) choose several and contact them early in the challenge process, and (2) develop a relationship with an individual at each organization you choose to work with by keeping them updated with challenge events. It becomes important to be able to pick up the phone and talk with someone on a first-name basis who is knowledgeable about your situation and knows of appropriate resources.

Our suggestion is that you start with your own professional organizations—ASCA and ACA—and add one or two that are primarily focused on censorship such as People For the American Way, National Coalition Against Censorship and the Education Commission of the States. After establishing ties with these organizations, your district's needs may lead you to others.

The following organizations have long and successful histories in helping educators defend against unwarranted attacks to curriculum materials and program. Many school counselors have reported how helpful and reassuring it was to be able to talk with someone who was knowledgeable about the censorship process and who could provide materials to help defend against a challenge.

American School Counselor Association
5999 Stevenson Avenue
Alexandria, VA 22304

Contact: Scott Swerling
(703) 823-9800, Ext. 387

American Civil Liberties Union
132 W. 43rd Street
New York, NY 10036
Contact: Alan Reitman

(212) 944-9800

Education Commission of the States
707 17th Street, Suite 27000
Denver, CO 80202

Contact: Arlene Arnsparger
(303) 299-3600

National Coalition Against Censorship
132 W. 43rd Street
New York, NY 10036

Contact: Leanne Katz
(212) 944-9899

American Counseling Association
5999 Stevenson Ave.
Alexandria, VA 22304

Contact: Carol Neiman
(703) 823-9800, Ext. 288

American Association of School Administrators
1801 N. Moore Street
Arlington, VA 22209

Contact: Gary Marx
(703) 528-0700

National Education Association
1201 16th Street NW
Washington, DC 20036

Contact: Paul Putnam
(202) 833-4000

People For the American Way
2000 M Street NW, St. 400
Washington, DC 20036

Contact: Field Department
(202) 467-4999 or
Mark Sedway
(800) 326-PFAW

Resources

This section lists resources for managing a curriculum challenge under the categories of key articles, important books and booklets, helpful newsletters, research and tips from publishers, and staying up-to-date.

Key Articles

National School Boards Association

- Harrington-Lueker. (1991). Book battles. *The American School Board Journal,* Vol. 178 (12), pp. 18-21, 37.
- Morris. (1992). Pressure groups and the politics of education. *Updating School Board Policies,* Vol. 23 (9), pp. 1-5.
- Jones. (1993). Targets of the right: Public school and school boards are under attack from the religious right. *The American School Board Journal,* Vol. 180 (4), pp. 22-29.

American Association of School Administrators

- The entire October, 1993 issue of *The School Administrator* focused on the growing influence of Far Right religious organizations on public education.

PTA

- *National PTA's guide to extremism* from the National PTA, 700 North Rush Street, Chicago, IL 60611-2571, (312) 787-0977.
- Fege (1991, March). Censorship in the schools: Parents can protect the freedom to learn, *PTA Today,* pp. 10-12.

Hatch Amendment Articles:

- Kaplan, L., and Geoffroy, K. (1987). The Hatch Amendment: A primer for counselors, Part I. *The School Counselor,* 34, pp. 9-16.
- Kaplan, L., and Geoffroy, K. (1987). The Hatch Amendment: A primer for counselors, part II. *The School Counselor,* 35, pp. 88-95.

Phi Delta Kappan

- McCarthy, M. M. (1993). Challenges to the public school curriculum: New targets and strategies. *Phi Delta Kappan,* Vol. 75 (1), pp. 55-60.

American Counseling Association

- McCullough, L. (1993, 1994). Challenges to guidance programs: A three part series on right wing challenges to school counseling programs. *Guidepost,* Vol. 36, (6,7,8).

Important Books and Booklets

The following two books are by Janet L. Jones and published by the Washington Education Association and the National Education Association, 33434 8th Street Avenue South, Federal Way, WA 98003, (800) 622-3393.

- *What's left after the right: A resource manual for educators* (1990).
- *No right turn: Assuring the forward progress of education reform* (1993).

The following three booklets are from People For the American Way, 2000 M Street N.W., Suite 400, Washington, DC 20036, (800) 326-7329.

- *The new target: Far right attacks on self-esteem programs* (1992).
- *Attacks on the freedom to learn* (1992).
- *Protecting the freedom to learn* (1989).

Other Important Books

- American Library Association and American Association of School Administrators. (1988). *Censorship and selection: Issues and answers for schools*. Chicago, IL: American Library Association, and American Association of School Administrators.
- Ochoa, A. (Ed.). (1990). *Academic freedom to teach and learn: Every teacher's issue*. Washington, DC: National Education Association.
- Peterson, M.P., and Poppen (1993). *School counselors and the first freedom*. Greensboro, NC: ERIC.

Helpful Newsletters

People For the American Way publish two newsletters covering censorship issues:

- *Right-Wing Watch*
- *Forum*

The American Library Association publishes a bi-monthly newsletter:

- *Newsletter on Intellectual Freedom*.

Research and Tips from Publishers

The following three programs are frequently challenged. They are also widely used and respected and represent key components of all developmental counseling, i.e., social skills, decision making, problem solving and self-esteem. The respective companies publishing these programs have lots of information to help counselors educate their publics about the programs.

PUMSY

- Timberline Press, P.O. Box 70187, Eugene, OR 97401, (503) 345-1771.

DUSO

- Karen Dahlen, Associate Director, El-Hi Publishing. American Guidance Service, Inc. 4201 Woodland Road, Circle Pines, MN 55014-1796, (800) 328-2560 Ext. 260.

QUEST

- Quest International, 537 Jones Road, P.O. Box 566, Granville, OH 43023-0566, (800) 466-2700.

Staying Up-to-Date

Because of the fast pace of events and decisions, it is important to stay current on the topics of censorship and challenges to school counseling and related programs. One way is to keep in touch with some of the helpful organizations listed in this chapter. ASCA and ACA for example, have a national network that is constantly updating available information on these issues. Secondly, if a challenge occurs in your district involving a published program, the publisher is a good source of relevant and current information. Finally, ERIC offers an index to articles and other publications which is broad and current. Information on contacting ASCA, ACA, and publishers is located earlier in this chapter. You may contact ERIC at (800) USE-ERIC.

Chapter 8

Fundamentalism and the Schools

by
Robert P. Green, Jr.

- Key Points

- Introduction: A Fundamentalist Complaint

- Fundamentalism and Modernism

- An Epistemological Debate

- History Lessons

- Fundamentalism and the Schools

- Implications for Educators

- A Final Note: Turning the Table

Dr. Robert P. Green, Jr. is an educational historian and a professor in the College of Education at Clemson University, Clemson, South Carolina.

Introduction to Chapter 8

Many counselors faced with a challenge to some guidance material or program that is being used are surprised to find that the same materials they find so useful, helpful, and important to working with young people can cause such pronounced discontent on the part of the challenger(s). Counselors frequently feel personally attacked. They often feel their intentions, values, and commitment to help children are being questioned.

The authors felt it was important to provide an historical summary of the thinking that underlies many of the challenges to school programs, and the implications of this thinking for educators. We asked Dr. Robert P. Green, Jr., who has studied the fundamentalist movement for over a decade, to provide background information.

Chapter 8 offers an explanation of the roots, methods of thinking, and legal approaches of a group that has been most vocal in its opposition to many current developmental guidance and counseling materials and programs. Professor Green attempts to explore the motives of these "challengers" and suggest the problems inherent in their position—philosophically, religiously, historically, and with reference to contemporary schools.

Chapter 8

Fundamentalism and the Schools

by
Robert P. Green, Jr.

Key Points

1. The term fundamentalist can be traced back to the early part of the twentieth century and the reaction of some evangelical theologians to "higher criticism" of the Bible.

2. Fundamentalists reject modernism (autonomous individualism with its rationalism, relativism, pluralism, and secularism) as undermining God, his revelations, and his prescriptions. They see themselves as the "last-ditch defenders of God."

3. Fundamentalists are involved in a revolution that affirms religious authority as holistic and absolute.

4. The fundamentalist reliance on the Bible as inerrant leads to flawed, *a priori* reasoning.

5. History lessons reveal these flaws.

6. Fundamentalists attempt to use the First Amendment's Establishment clause in two ways: They argue that certain materials interfere with their free expression of religion, and they argue that the use of certain materials promotes particular religious views (e.g. "secular humanism" and/or "New Age").

7. To date, the federal courts have rejected their interpretations. Said Judge William Shubb: "The Establishment clause is not violated merely because a particular governmental sponsored activity happens to coincide or harmonize with the tenets of some or all religions."

8. Educators have a responsibility to prepare children for the real world, to pass along our cultural and scientific heritage. Much of that knowledge is humanistic, and it is certainly secular.

9. Materials used in some fundamentalist schools would be unacceptable to the vast majority of Americans.

Introduction: A Fundamentalist Complaint

It is late summer, 1992 and a religious fundamentalist addresses a meeting of the school board of a small, rural Southern county. The county's use of the *PUMSY* elementary guidance program is being challenged on the grounds that it reflects aspects of New Age religion. He begins by explaining why Christian (well, some Christians, he admits, but one suspects he means *real* Christian) are upset over programs like that in which "Pumsy" plays a role. He claims that "We can't pray" in schools and the Supreme Court has even banned the posting of the Ten Commandments on classroom walls because "students might read the Ten Commandments, then go out and obey them, and that would be unconstitutional!"

While Christianity is being removed from the schools, he argues, other religions—New Age religions—are creeping in. As evidence of some weird Earth-worship promoted by the schools, he cites an environmentally conscious adaptation of the Pledge of Allegiance ("I Pledge allegiance to the Earth/And all the life which it supports..." [1]) which, he claims, students in Maine schools recite *instead* of the national pledge!

Even if there were no New Age threat, he can't believe that "liberal educators" defend "junk" like that in the *PUMSY* program. He cites a survey of research that found "no support" for claims that "parapsychology, neurolinguistics, and integration of left and right brain hemispheres" improve learning.

Finally, he reads a relaxation passage "directly from the teacher's manual." The passage asks students to relax and imagine a beautiful and peaceful field with a pond. It states that students can return to this peaceful place whenever they want to. In other words, "imagine this place when you need to relax." Innocuous? Certainly not, for this passage reflects "physical monism," and physical monism leads to the idea that "you can create your own reality"!

The presentation is punctuated with sighs, gasps of concern, and periodic "Amen's" from supporters in the audience. *Yet the presentation is characterized by simplistic renderings of the Supreme Court's attempts to define separation of church and state. It is character-*

ized by skewed information. Can an individual pray during school-time? Of course he or she can. The Supreme Court has attempted to deal with *state-supported prayer*, not individual prayer. Was the Court (in *Stone v. Graham*) implying that an individual's decision to obey the Ten Commandments was unconstitutional? Of course not. Does Maine require its students to pledge allegiance to the Earth? No. Is the *PUMSY* program based on or does it incorporate any of the approaches criticized in the survey of research cited by the activist above? No. *PUMSY* does, however, use relaxation strategies—and the same study found that relaxation may, indeed, be beneficial.[2] Is *PUMSY* promoting alternative realities? Of course not.

Despite the flawed nature of this presentation, it rings true to many in the audience. While this event took place in a rural Southern county, the same scene is being played out across the country. Members of the fundamentalist Christian Right are becoming more and more active in public schools. Why? What is the nature of their concern, the basis for their thinking? Why do so many seemingly innocuous aspects of contemporary schooling appear so threatening to these people? The answer lies in the contemporary, fundamentalist Christian rejection of modernism.

Fundamentalism and Modernism

In order to explain the anxiety with which fundamentalists view many current educational practices (e.g. those they label "New Age" or "humanistic"—that is, beginning with man rather than God), it is necessary to review the historical roots of fundamentalism and its contemporary expressions. The use of the term fundamentalist can be traced back to the early twentieth century and the reaction of a number of evangelical theologians to then current developments in theology. The views of these conservative theologians appeared in a series of volumes entitled *The Fundamentals*. A central development against which they reacted grew out of modern Biblical criticism. Scholars had attempted to adapt modern methods of thinking, including methods of historical and literary criticism, to their studies of the Bible. One result was that many theologians began to question—and reject—literal interpretations of the Bible. Their studies of the Bible revealed such things as inconsistencies in translation through various versions of the Bible, passages ascribed to one author which must have been written by many, common themes between Biblical passages and elements of pagan religions, and so on—all casting doubt on the idea that the King James Version, for example, was the literal word of God. (It must be noted that these studies did not reduce the faith of most of these scholars in the "truths" contained in the Bible. For example, despite the fact that they might have labeled the Genesis account of creation as "religious myth," that account nevertheless provided insights into the nature of man and his relationship to God. A modern Biblical Scholar, however, would not accept the story as an historical account. [3]) In reaction to this development, a major tenet of the fundamentalists was—and is—Biblical inerrancy. "God has preserved the Scriptures for us so that they have remained unadulterated, by which we mean free from error," argued one literalist. Despite the numerous translations through which Holy Scripture passed, God, through miraculous intervention, had guaranteed the literal truth of "every sentence, every word, every syllable, every letter" in the Bible. Furthermore, even if reason and observation conflicted with the Biblical account—as did, for example, scientific evidence for the age of the Earth and the evolution of life forms— the Bible retained the truth of the matter. Human observation and reason were inadequate sources of information about the nature of reality: "man, because of sin, has been so blinded that he cannot read the divine script in nature."[4]

Biblical inerrancy is the heart of the contemporary fundamentalists' critique of modern society. According to Francis A. Schaeffer, intellectual father of contemporary fundamentalism, liberal theology with its higher criticism has succumbed to "rationalism." That is, the belief that "man can understand the universe by beginning from himself without any recourse to outside knowledge, specifically outside knowledge or revelation from God."[5] The development of rationalism is traced by Schaeffer and other fundamentalist thinkers to the Enlightenment and the Scientific Revolution.[6] Yet to them, the path of rationalism has been a dead-end street. Rationalism leads only to pessimism. Humans find themselves as insignificant parts of a meaningless machine. Modern rationalism leads humankind to believe "that there is no final truth, no meaning, no absolutes, that it is not only that we have not found truth and meaning, but that they do not exist."[7]

For the fundamentalist, however, there is a unified concept of knowledge and life, there are absolutes, there is final truth. These absolutes and this final truth are revealed in the Bible, "The Bible and Christ in His office of prophet have given a propositional, verbalized communication to men that is true about God, true about history, and true about the cosmos," writes Schaeffer.[8] Acceptance of the Biblical message provides escape from the "cosmic alienation" of modern humankind.

The intellectual foundation for this concept of unified knowledge and life is the inerrant Bible. Again and again, Schaeffer en-
dorses the historical view of Christianity that "the original writings
of the Bible were so inspired by God as to be kept free from error."[9]
The Bible provides "an objective and absolute standard."[10] This
being the case, "Bible-believing Christians" must practice what
Schaeffer calls "antithesis." "We must act upon, witness, and preach
this fact: what is contrary to God's revealed propositional truth is
not true."[11]

Schaeffer recognizes that fundamentalist Christians are in a
minority. He feels, and other fundamentalists agree, that the record
of modernity shows growing repression of fundamentalist belief. "I
believe the church is in real danger," he writes. "It is in for a rough
day. We are racing present pressures and a present and future
manipulation which will be so overwhelming in the days to come
that they will make the battles of the last forty years look like child's
play."[12] Furthermore, "the world is on fire."

*We are not only losing the church, but our entire culture as well.
We live in the post-Christian world which is under the judgment
of God. I believe today that we must speak as Jeremiah... I believe
that we of Northern Europe since the Reformation have had such
light as few others have ever possessed. We have stamped upon
that light in our culture. Our cinemas, our novels, our art muse-
ums scream out as they stamp upon that light. And worst of all,
modern theology screams out as it stamps upon that light....*[13]

Yet Schaeffer does not despair. Rather, he calls for a "Christian
Revolution" based upon "the preaching and practice of truth."

*We do not need 51 percent of the American population to begin
to have an influence. If 20 percent of the American population
were really regenerate Christians, clear about their doctrines,
beliefs and values, taking truth seriously, taking a consistent
position, we could begin, not to have an overwhelming consensus, but at least to have a vital voice again in the midst of our
community.*[14]

It is this call for Christian Revolution that motivates the fundamentalist Christians today. In fact, religious historian Bruce B.
Lawrence defines fundamentalism as "the affirmation of religious
authority as holistic and absolute, admitting of neither criticism nor
reduction; it is expressed through the collective demand that specific creedal and ethical dictates derived from scripture be *publicly
recognized and legally enforced.*"[15] [Italics added]

[Fundamentalism] is a series of revolts by those who uphold deep-seated religious values against what they perceive to be the shallow indeterminacy of modern ideologies. Rationalism or relativism, pluralism or secularism—each undermines the Divine Transcendent, challenging his revelations, denying his prophets, ignoring his morally guided community. Without certainty the world is doomed. With it salvation (for some) is assured. The righteous remnant are emissaries of an All-Powerful, All-Knowing Being who has been betrayed by the freedom he granted the modern age. Who are the fundamentalists? They are the last-ditch defenders of God.[16]

An Epistemological Debate

In many ways the debate between a fundamentalist view of the world and a modern, scientific view is a metaphysical debate, but it is certainly an epistemological debate, a debate over the source of knowledge or truth. It is also a debate over methods of reasoning about the truth. It has important implications for the public schools. It is a debate that Western society has held before.

Of course, when describing complex concepts such as belief and reasoning systems, it is easy to over-simplify; nevertheless, two distinct approaches will be described here. On the one side is the belief that knowledge and truth are revealed to man. Universal principles are manifestations of God's mind and are revealed through the Bible. On the other side is the belief that man must observe nature and derive principles from that observation. *Despite the claims of Francis Schaeffer and other fundamentalists, many modern thinkers do not see the two as necessarily mutually exclusive.* At any rate, two basic methods of reasoning can be associated with the two positions described.

The method of reasoning based on revealed truth is deductive in nature. Deductive logic is reasoning from general principles to specifics. Its classical representation is the deductive syllogism—composed of a major premise, a minor premise, and a conclusion: All humans are mortal (major premise). Socrates is a human (minor premise). Therefore, Socrates is mortal (conclusion). The reasoning is from the general to the specific because one begins with a general principle ("All humans are mortal") and applies it to a specific situation (Socrates) in order to derive a conclusion. Traditional Christian thought pursues just his method, but with the principles or major premises derived from the Bible. This method of reasoning, however, is not that of modern science.

The method of modern science is basically inductive in nature. Inductive reasoning is reasoning from the specific to the general. With inductive reasoning, observations are made and common aspects of those observations form the basis for generalizations. These generalizations can then be used to both predict and explain. For example, meteorologists observe atmospheric conditions in order to predict the weather. Thousands and thousands of observations in the past have led meteorologists to generalize: given certain atmospheric conditions, rain is likely. In some areas of scientific inquiry, generalizations are more accurate than others. But the process is the same: observation of natural phenomena leads to generalization about those phenomena, "scientific" knowledge. The process is the basis for modern science—physical, biological, social. It is a central aspect of modern life.

Perhaps the easiest way to perceive the nature of this debate is to look at one of the specific topics around which it revolves, the theory of evolution. On one side of the debate are proponents of creationism. They believe in the Biblical account of creation and argue that it, as simply another theory, should be given equal time in the classroom. They have even coined the term "creation science." Many scientists, on the other hand, point out that a scientific theory is based upon inductive reasoning, generalization derived from observation of natural phenomena. Creationism, then, is not a scientific theory. It is not constructed in the same way. Creationism is based upon *a priori* truths. That is, the Biblical account is accepted as truth, and evidence is then sought to confirm it.

Now, of course, deductive reasoning based upon *a priori* principles in certainly a valid and useful method. The U.S. Supreme Court uses this method, for example, when it considers the constitutionality of an action or piece of legislation. That is, given a constitutional principle, the court applies that principle to a specific situation (law or government action) to determine the constitutionality of that law or action. This is what the court did in a recent case involving a Louisiana law mandating balanced treatment for the theories of evolution and creation in that state's public schools. The Court began with the constitutional principle of separation of church and state (First Amendment). Given that principle, the Court applied it to the Louisiana case. The majority of the justices viewed the Louisiana law as a violation of the principle, so it was declared unconstitutional.[17] *The difference between this application of deductive reasoning and its application by fundamentalists, however, must be noted. In Court cases and other secular applications of deductive reason-*

ing, both the major and minor premises are susceptible to critical review; that is, they can be challenged for adequacy, accuracy, and so forth. Recently, for example, the Supreme Court found in *Lamb's Chapel v. Center Moriches Union Free School District* that after-hours religious events in public schools that allow a variety of after-hours community events do not violate the principle of separation.[18] In the view of fundamentalists, on the other hand, Biblical statements are not susceptible to critical review and cannot be modified. They are perceived as inerrant. But the teaching of ideas based upon unchallengeable, revealed truth poses serious problems for public school teachers.

Schools and textbooks must function to prepare children for life in the real world. The school's job is to pass along the culture's knowledge. *Acquiescing to complaints from fundamentalists concerning information presented in textbooks—information that they argue contravenes their religious beliefs—can, in fact, be dysfunctional for society.* What might happen if we were to accept the fundamentalist position concerning the Bible as a source of knowledge and the reasoning based upon *a priori* truth derived from that source? One cannot be sure, but certain lessons from history are instructive.

History Lessons

Evidence of the dysfunctional nature of reasoning based upon *a priori* truth is abundant in our history. One well-known example revolves around the observations of the famous Italian scientist Galileo (1564-1642) who published evidence in support of the Copernican theory of the universe. That is, that the Sun is the center of the universe. At that time, using deductive reasoning based upon *a priori* "truth," the Church argued that the earth was the center of the universe. Their fundamental assumption was that the Bible was literally true. There are any number of passages in the Bible which suggest that the earth is the center of the universe and that it does not move around anything: "The world also is established, that it cannot be moved" (Psalm 93:1); "Who laid the foundations of the earth, that it should not be moved forever" (Psalm 104:5). One observer summarized the Biblical cosmology as follows:

> *The earth was flat and was founded on an underlying sea (Psalm 136:6; Psalm 24:1-2; Genesis 7:11); it was stationary; the heavens, like an upturned bowl, "strong as a molten mirror" (Job 37:18; Genesis 1:6-8; Isaiah 40:22; Psalm 104:2), rested on the*

earth beneath (Amos 9:6; Job 26:11); the sun, moon and stars moved within the firmament of special purpose to illumine man (Genesis 1:14-19); there was a sea above the sky, "the waters which were above the firmament" (Genesis 7:11; Psalm 78:23)....[19]

Thus, Church spokesmen argued, the Sun must be moving around the earth—not the other way around. Their reasoning: The Bible is literally true, the Bible says the earth is the center of the universe, therefore the earth is the center of the universe. Galileo, of course, based his argument that the earth revolved around the Sun on empirical evidence, telescopic observations. Hauled before the Inquisition, he was forced to recant his position. It is, of course, silly to ask which version of reality should be taught in schools today.

The story of medieval maps is yet another example of the problems inherent in accepting *a priori* truths and reasoning based upon them. At least as early as the fifth century B.C., Greek scholars had reasoned that, despite appearances to the individual, the earth was round. The ancient geographer Eratosthenes (ca. 276-195 B.C.) even derived a remarkably accurate figure for the circumference of the earth based upon observation and calculation. Historian Daniel Boorstin tells the story:

From travelers Eratosthenes had heard that at noon on June 21 the sun cast no shadow in a well at Syene (modern Aswan) and was thus directly overhead. He knew that the sun always cast a shadow at Alexandria. From knowledge available to him he considered Syene to be due south of Alexandria. The idea occurred to him that if he could measure the length of the shadow of the sun in Alexandria at the time when there was no shadow in Aswan, he could calculate the circumference of the earth. On June 21 he measured the shadow of an obelisk in Alexandria and by simple geometry he calculated that the sun was 7°14' from overhead. This is one-fiftieth of the 360° that make a full circle. This measure was remarkably accurate for the actual difference in latitude of Aswan and Alexandria, by our best modern calculation, is 7°14'. Thus, the circumference of the earth was fifty times the distance from Syene to Alexandria. But how great was this distance? From travelers he learned that camels needed 50 days to cover the trip and that a camel traveled 100 stadia in a day. The distance from Syene to Alexandria was thus calculated at 5,000 stadia (50 x 100). He then calculated the circumference of the earth to be 250,000 stadia (50 x 5,000). We are not sure about the conversion of stadia (originally 600 Greek feet) into modern measures, but the best estimates put the Greek stadium at about 607 feet.... By this calculation Eratosthenes arrived at a figure for the circumference of the earth of some 28,700 miles....[20]

In the second century B.C., Hipparchus of Nicaea (c. 165-127 B.D.) developed a gridwork system of latitude and longitude lines, points along the lines to be established with reference to celestial phenomena. In the process, Hipparchus divided the earth into 360 "degrees"—about 70 miles along the equator, which gave us the "degree" of the modern geographer. Later, Ptolemy (A.D. 90-168) improved upon Hipparchus' grid system, popularized the expressions for latitude and longitude, and subdivided Hipparchus' degrees into minutes and seconds.

Yet what happened to Greek observation and reasoning during the Middle Ages, when the minds of Western Europeans fell under the protection of the Church? It was replaced by Christian dogma, a dogma which declared that the earth was flat. The thought that anyone existed at the "Antipodes" (the other side of the earth, where men's feet were opposite) was rejected out of hand: "Can anyone be so foolish," wrote the Christian Lactantius, "as to believe that there are men whose feet are higher than their heads, or places where things may be hanging downwards, trees growing backwards, or rain falling upwards? Where is the marvel of the hanging gardens of Babylon if we are to allow of a hanging world at the Antipodes?" "God forbid," wrote another, "that anybody think we accept the stories of antipodes, which are in every way contradictory to Christian faith." In fact, belief in "Antipodes" became a common charge against heretics.[21]

Rejecting, or unaware of, Greek contributions to our understanding of the globe, Christian theologians came up with their own maps—maps derived from Scripture. At the center of these maps was Jerusalem. "Thus saith the Lord God; This is Jerusalem: I have set it in the midst of the nations and countries that are round about her" (Ezekiel 5:5). Historian Boorstin describes the maps:

The whole habitable earth was depicted as a circular dish... divided by a T-shaped flow of water. East was put at the top, which was what was then meant by "orienting" a map. Above the "T" was the continent of Asia, below to the left of the vertical was the continent of Europe, and to the right was Africa. The bar dividing Europe from Africa is the Mediterranean Sea; the horizontal bar dividing Europe and Africa from Asia is the Danube and the Nile, supposed to flow in a single line. All is surrounded by the "Ocean Sea."[22]

Christian maps may have been faithful depictions of Biblical images. They were, however, worthless to navigators. The flat earth and medieval map are rejected today because of knowledge based on observation. Thus, a modern philosopher such as Mortimer J. Adler, by no means an advocate of what he calls "the dogmatic materialism of a great many scientists," argues: "No article of faith should remain firm among the dogmas of the Church if what it claims to be true runs counter to what we know by other means and methods.... An interpretation [of Holy Scripture] cannot be true or is seriously doubtful if it conflicts with what, at a given time, we know through science either beyond the shadow of doubt or beyond a reasonable doubt."[23]

Fundamentalism and the Schools

Traditionally, American public schools have been responsive to demands from the public, and the socialization and training of the young is a sensitive and significant area for society as well as parents. It should be no surprise, then, that the fundamentalist revolt against modernism focuses in part on schools, their curricula and instructional materials. The school, or at least the school board-room, becomes one battlefield in that revolt. For the fundamentalist, manifestations of modern malaise need to be rooted out—at least their children need be protected from them. Their efforts have taken the form of both political and legal action. Examples of the latter are instructive.

In general, fundamentalists have used the First Amendment to the Constitution as the basis for their efforts to shape school policy and materials. That amendment states, with respect to religion, that "Congress shall make no law respecting an establishment of religion, or prohibiting the free exercise thereof..." The congressional prohibition is extended to the states (and thus to their public schools) through the Fourteenth Amendment, which states, "No state shall make or enforce any law which shall abridge the privileges or immunities of citizens of the United States." In essence, with reference to public schools, the Supreme Court has interpreted these amendments in ways to avoid entanglement between the states' schools and religion. That is, the courts have attempted to restrict situations that give the appearance of school support for a particular religious view or views.[24]

Fundamentalists have adapted this principle in two ways: First, they argue that some instructional materials interfere with their free exercise of religion by undermining articles of their faith, and second, that the schools, in fact, promote a particular religious view through the use of instructional materials that reflect the religions of secular humanism or New Age. In such cases the state is, in effect, establishing religion. *To date, the federal courts have rejected these interpretations, but not without some successes for fundamentalists at the district court level. A few examples will be illustrative.*

The case of *Mozert, et. al v. Hawkins County Public Schools et. al.* began in 1983, when parents of children in the Greenville, Tennessee, schools sued the school board of Hawkins County, arguing that the required reading series (Holt, Rinehart, and Winston) violated their religious beliefs by teaching evolution, secular humanism, the occult and other anti-religious ideas. The parents presented a list of over 300 objections to the court, including passages from *The Diary of Anne Frank* (which was said to have taught the idea that all religions are equal before God), *The Wizard of Oz* (which contradicted the Biblical lesson that all witches are bad), the works of anthropologist Margaret Mead, science and science fiction writer Isacc Asimov, and fairy-tale writer Hans Christian Andersen. District Judge Thomas Hull found that certain texts did propound ideas antithetical to the religious beliefs of some students. Those students, he argued, should have been provided with alternative materials. In appeal, however, the 6th. Circuit Court failed to see the anti-Christian nature of the Holt reading materials: "[The] plaintiffs appeared to assume that material clearly presented as poetry, fiction and even 'make-believe' in the Holt series were presented as facts which the students were required to believe. Nothing in the record supports this assumption." Furthermore, the Court rejected the plaintiff's appeal to the First Amendment: "The requirement that students read the assigned materials and attend reading classes, in the absence of a showing that this participation entailed affirmation or denial of a religious belief... does not place an unconstitutional burden on the students' exercise of religion...."[25]

The case of *Smith et. al. v. Board of School Commissioners of Mobile County* was created in August 1985 by District Judge W.B. Hand when he reorganized an earlier case that had been remanded to his court.[26] Smith and other parents sought an injunction against the Mobile schools on the grounds that they were teaching the "religions of secularism, humanism, evolution, materialism, agnosticism, atheism and others."[27] Special concern was expressed over material in home economics and social studies textbooks. Hand found that certain of these texts taught the religion of secular humanism, thus running afoul of the Constitutional prohibition against the establishment of a state religion. He ordered the removal of the offending texts from the state's classrooms. On appeal, the 11th Circuit Court reversed Hand's ban of the social studies and home economics texts. While the Court declined to state whether or not secular humanism was a religion, it argued that even if secular humanism were a religion, it was not shown that Alabama promoted it through the use of texts under question. "Examination of the contents of these textbooks... reveals that the message conveyed is not one of endorsement of secular humanism or any religion," wrote Circuit Judge Frank Johnson, Jr. "Rather, the message conveyed is one of a governmental attempt to instill in Alabama public school children such values as independent thought, tolerance of diverse views, self-respect, maturity, self-reliance and logical decision-making." With reference to the social studies texts, which plaintiffs argued had failed to adequately portray the role of religion in American development, the judges stated that there was nothing to indicate that "omission of certain facts regarding religion from these textbooks of itself constituted an advancement of secular humanism or an active hostility towards a theistic religion." According to the Court, the textbooks neither endorsed nor discredited theistic religion as a system of belief. "Indeed, many of the books specifically acknowledge that religion is one source of moral values and none preclude that possibility."[28]

More recently, in the 1992 case of *Brown v. Woodland Joint Unified School District*, fundamentalist parents challenged the use of the "Impression" elementary reading series. "Impression" is a literature-based reading series that includes work from such writers as A.A. Milne, Martin Luther King, Jr., Madeline L'Engel, Laura Ingalls Wilder, Dr. Seuss, Rudyard Kipling, and C.S. Lewis. The plaintiffs argued that references to witches, ghosts, and goblins in the stories and activities promoted the religions of witchcraft and neo-paganism, thus violating the establishment clause of the First Amendment. District Judge William Shubb rejected the claims of the plaintiffs, pointing out that witches are common characters in children's literature and folklore and that, in literature, myths and folk stories are often used to make philosophical points or instruct children concerning non-religious matters. *In short, he argued, "The Establishment Clause is not violated merely because a particular governmental sponsored activity happens to coincide or harmonize with the tenets of some or all religions."*[29]

Interestingly, these cases reflect the contemporary use among fundamentalists of the flawed *a priori* reasoning discussed above. The belief in a secular humanist or New Age plot is an unshakable part of the fundamentalist view of the world. It can be seen in the relatively low-key work of James Hitchcock, who argued that certain pressure groups after World War II, "had a vision of a secularized America, and they planned and executed a judicial and legal strategy to have that vision enshrined in law."[30] It can also be seen in the burning rhetoric of popular fundamentalist writer Texe Marrs:

> *A deadly and evil cold wind is viciously blowing with magnum force across America and the globe. From whence does it come? The Bible reveals that Satan is the* hellish creator *of this rough and chilling air current. He is the "prince of the power of the air" (Eph. 2:2). But the gale force winds now ripping through man's weakened defenses and shaking the very foundations of the world also have an* earthly source: *the New Age Movement....*

> *Satan knows his days are numbered. He must do his evil work quickly while there is still time, for soon Jesus Christ, King of Kings and Lord of Lords, will arrive on Planet Earth. Like a mighty whirlwind from heaven He will seize the Kingdom promised Him by the Father from the beginning and destroy the Adversary and his legions of followers. God's will shall prevail...*

> *The immediate future will be bleak for all of humanity. The Christian community will especially be in jeopardy as New Age leaders, incited by their demonic overlords, ruthlessly and methodically carry out their meticulously prepared Plan for world domination. Satan has energized his followers with a special infusion of enthusiasm and ill will. The planet will experience uncontrollable spasms of violence and chaos. Widespread terror and rampant savagery will envelop the land, and blood will be shed on a massive scale.*[31]

Given the idea of some kind of plot as Truth, it is not hard to find evidence to back it up. Picture, if you will, the analytical process. *A fundamentalist reviewer—convinced that secular humanist or New Age plots exist—reads through a book looking for passages that reflect anything that might be interpreted as anti-family, anti-authority, anti-Christian. This never fails to generate a long list of offensive passages (often taken out of context and many pages apart).* The plaintiff's exhibits in *Smith*, for example, included offensive passages such as the following: "Specialists in human development classify growth or development as physical, social, emotional, and intellectual." "According to Maslow, physical needs have first priority." "One hundred years ago, there was one divorce for every thirty-four marriages. Divorce was considered a sin against God. Many people thought it immoral and an indication of a weak or poor character." "If you decide to accept the demanding role of mother or father, you will face many value choices. And you will be responsible for helping your children form worthwhile values for their lives." "While smoking is a matter of individual choice, most authorities now agree that it is preferable never to smoke." "Understanding your own values will help you set satisfying goals." "A single man or woman who sets up a household can also be called a family."[32] *Passages such as these may appear innocuous to the non-believer. For the fundamentalist, however, they provide unmistakable and sinister evidence that supports their presuppositions. Applying the same reasoning in the Brown case, we see: Satan's New Age plot uses demons and witches to achieve his ends (major premise). There are witches in this literature anthology (minor premise). Therefore, this literature anthology promotes Satan's New Age and violates my religious rights (conclusion).*

In the literature on logical thinking, this flawed line of reasoning is sometimes called "confirmatory bias," the tendency to seek out information that confirms one's premise. As logician T. Gilovich argues, "When trying to assess whether a belief is valid, people tend to seek out information that would confirm the belief over information that might disconfirm it." Among logicians, this is recognized as one of the most common kinds of errors in reasoning.[33]

Implications for Educators

The implications of fundamentalists' rejection of aspects of modern life and their proscription of materials based upon *a priori* reasoning are problematic, at best, for educators. While public schools must be responsive to public concerns, and fundamentalists are part of that public, they also must educate children for the real world. *Suppose, for example, that the logic of District Judge Thomas Hull in Mozert (that is, children should be released from lessons that offend their Christian beliefs) were extended to the teaching of geography. Should a student be allowed to leave the room to avoid hearing that the earth is round?* Apparently, given Judge Hull's logic. Certainly, argued Jim Cooper, education liaison to Arizona's recent governor, Evan Mecham. Speaking before a legislative committee in the 1980s in defense of a bill that would require the teaching of creationism in Arizona schools, Cooper asserted that a student had the right to believe that the earth is flat and that "a teacher would have to acknowledge [that] right" as long as the belief was part of the child's religion.[34] *The potential for disruption of the educational process as a result of this line of reasoning is mind-boggling!*

One might argue, of course, that the above example is silly, that the question of the shape of the earth is hardly one that would be questioned from a religious standpoint today. Yet one of the complaints of the plaintiffs in *Mozert* was that an excerpt from the *Wizard of Oz* "taught" that there were both good and bad witches, contrary to the Biblical description of witches as bad. Or, consider the complaint in *Brown*, that references in the "Impressions" literature series to witches, ghosts, and goblins in the stories and activities promoted the religions of witchcraft and neo-paganism. One has a difficult time figuring how today's hard-pressed public school teachers would be able to come up with alternative materials for those who believe in such things as a flat earth and wicked witches!

As Donna Hulsizer of People For the American Way put it, "[M]ost of the topics considered objectionable [to fundamentalist Christians] are part of our human and cultural heritage, and they pervade education."

> *[I]magine an elementary classroom in which the teacher is faced with excusing even as few as five children from different religious backgrounds from different lessons because those lessons offend their religious beliefs. Is a teacher to do so every time an objectionable topic is mentioned, even in passing?... When parents' objections are so broadly defined, teachers will need to become amateur theologians to determine what might offend the beliefs of these students....*
>
> *The chilling effect... may spill over into teaching as well, with teachers avoiding controversial subjects and shying away from activities such as open-ended questions, debate and role play (also a target of objections under the secular humanism label) that make instruction vivid and engaging for students.*[45]

Fortunately, the effect of court opinions to date reinforces the public school's foundation as purveyor of the knowledge of the culture. Much of that knowledge is humanistic, and it is certainly secular. The inability of the public schools to teach information that has either—or both—characteristic would prove a disservice to society.

A Final Note: Turning the Table

Given the range of materials that fall under fundamentalists' proscriptions, one is led to wonder what kinds of materials they do advocate. The answer is interesting, if one assumes—logically enough—that textbooks used in some fundamentalist Christian schools pass muster. Turning the table on the techniques of fundamentalists, a recent study by Doerr and Menendez of literature and history textbooks used in some Christian schools and published by fundamentalist institutions reveals some interesting pieces and patterns of information as well as some unusual views of history:

- The Catholic Church, to which more Americans belong than any other, "enslaves man," is a "wicked, corrupted system which insured the people's intellectual and spiritual ignorance by depriving them of God's infallible word," and "destroyed more Bibles than the pagan emperors." Catholic teachings and practices are continually labeled "blasphemous" and "pagan," and the contributions of Catholics to U.S. and European history are downplayed, ignored, or distorted.

- The Episcopal Church... is repeatedly ridiculed. It and its sister, the Church of England, are "dead in ritualism and rationalism," "serve mainly a ceremonial function," have lost their "scriptural authority," and "without constitutional safeguard would destroy evangelical churches." We are told that "such religion had little effect upon upper-class morality and left the masses little better than barbarians."

- The Quakers are "unbiblical" and "dangerous to biblical Christianity."

- The Mormon Church is a "cult." The proliferation of many religions in a nation that cherishes religious freedom is seen as a threat. "All these false versions of true religion and worship contribute to the growing theological anarchy of a nation whose people do merely what seems right in their own eyes...."

- One reason for the Civil War was the South's desire to preserve its Protestant identify. (In fact, both North and South were predominantly Protestant, and Jefferson Davis' Cabinet, unlike that of Lincoln, included Catholics and Jews....)

- Black Americans are treated with relative indifference and are always referred to as negroes, even in 1991 editions. Students are reminded that "the Bible does not specifically condemn slavery...."

- The United Nations is "unbiblical...."
- Labor unions "create turmoil" and fail "to govern the greed of their members." Furthermore, "most of the major labor strikes in our history have been immoral.[36]

Doerr and Menendez warn that, should voucher plans become reality, American taxpayers might be subsidizing indoctrination and bigotry. The fundamentalist Rev. Tim LaHaye includes the following publications, groups and organizations in his list of liberal humanist thinkers (and thus supporters of atheism, evolution, and amorality): *Time, Life, NBC, ABC, CBS,* N.O.W., liberal Democrats, liberal Republicans, socialists, communists, the American Bar Association, the NAACP, liberal religions (Protestant, Catholic, and Jew), the National Council of Churches, the National Education Association leadership, and the list goes on.[37] Note the political and social nature of the list. Religious historian Bruce Lawrence describes fundamentalism as religious ideology, but one must decide for oneself whether fundamentalist Christians are perpetrating religion or simply ideology.

Notes

[1] This pledge appears on a poster copyrighted by Janina Lamb. The full text reads, "I pledge allegiance to the Earth and all the life which it supports. One planet, in our care. Irreplaceable, with sustenance and respect for all." C 1992 Janina Lamb. Lamb & Lion Studio. Box 298. Tarnworth, NH 03886.

[2] "News Briefs,' *Science News*, January 1988.

[3] An early statement of this position can be found in Harry Emerson Fosdick, "A Reply to Mr. Bryan in the Name of Religion," in Gail Kennedy (ed.), *Evolution and Religion* (Boston: D.C. Health & Co., 1957), pp. 30-34.

[4] Quoted in A. James Reichley, *Religion in American Public Life* (Washington, D.C.; The Brookings Institution, 1985), p. 206.

[5] Francis A. Schaeffer, *The Church at the End of the 20th Century with The Church Before the Watching World* (Westchester, Illinois: Crossway Books, 1985), p. 113.

[6] See, for example, James Hitchcock, *What is Secular Humanism?* (Servant Books: Ann Arbor, Michigan, 1982.)

[7] Schaeffer, p. 23.

[8] Ibid., p. 112.

[9] Ibid., p. 120.

[10] Ibid., p. 121

[11] Ibid., p. 40.

[12] Ibid., p. 5.

[13] Ibid., p. 154.

[14] Ibid., pp. 42-43.

[15] Bruce B. Lawrence, *Defenders of God: The Fundamentalist Revolt Against the Modern Age* (New York: Harper & Row, 1989), p. 27.

[16] Ibid., p. ix.

[17] Writing for the Court, Justice William Brennan argued that the purpose of the law was "clearly to advance the religious viewpoint that a supernatural being created humankind.... The legislative history documents that the act's primary purpose was to change the science curriculum of public schools in order to provide an advantage to a particular religious doctrine that rejects the factual basis of evolution in its entirety," he wrote in *Edwards v. Aguilard* (55 USLW 3058).

[18] "Religious Groups Win in Top court" (*The Greenville News*, June 8, 1993), p. 1.

[19] Fosdick, pp. 31-32.

[20] Daniel J. Boorstin, *The Discoverers: a History of Man's Search to Know His World and Himself* (New York: Vintage Books, 1985), pp. 95-98.

[21] Ibid., p. 107

[22] Ibid., p. 101

[23] Mortimer J. Adler, *Truth in Religion: The Plurality of Religions and the Unity of Truth* (New York: Macmillan, 1990), pp. 33-34. In this work, Adler criticizes contemporary expressions of the medieval Arabic philosopher Averroes's idea that truths of reason and truths of faith, although incompatible, could both be factually true. "Wherever the fruits of technology are used, the truth of mathematics and nature science are acknowledged," he argues, "...the schizophrenia resulting from an Averroistic duality of truth in the domains of science and religion... is not a healthy state of mind and should not be welcomed and embraced." See pp. 74-76.

[24] Archibald Cox, *The Court and the Constitution* (Boston: Houghton-Mifflin, 1987), pp. 198-208.

[25] "Appeals Court Overturns Tennessee Textbook Ruling, "*The Greenville News*, August 25, 1987.

[26] See *Wallace v. Jaffree*, 105 S. Ct. 2479 (1985)

[27] *Smith et. al. v. Board of School Commissioners of Mobile County*, U.S. District Court for the Southern District of Alabama, Southern Division, Mobile, Alabama, No. CIV-82-0544-BH, No. CIV-82-0792-BH, 1987.

[28] "Appeals Court Reverses Ban on Textbooks, "*The Greenville News*," August 27, 1987.

[29] "Brown v. Woodland Joint Unified School District: A Victory for Public Education and Free Expression" (People For the American Way Flyer, No Date), pp. 1-2.

[30] Hitchcock, p. 101.

[31] Texe Marrs, *Mystery Mark of the New Age: Satan's Design for World Domination* (Westchester Illinois: Crossway Books, 1988), pp. vii-viii.

[32] *Smith v. Board.*

[33] T. Gilovich, *How We Know What Isn't So* (New York: Free Press, 1991), p. 33.

[34] "People," *Education Week*, February 18, 1987, p. 5.

[35] Donna Hulsizer, "Public Education on Trial," *Educational Leadership*, Vol. 44, No. 8, May 1987, p. 16.

[36] Edd Doerr and Albert J. Menendez, "Should Tax Dollars Subsidize Bigotry?" *Phi Delta Kappan*, Vol. 74, No. 2, October 1992, pp. 165-167.

[37] Rev. Tim LaHaye, "The Religion of Secular Humanism" in Stanley M. Elam, ed. *Public Schools and the First Amendment* (Indianapolis, Indiana: Phi Delta Kappa, 1982), p. 5.

Appendix A
Sample Policy on Selection of School Counseling Materials

The primary objective of selecting materials is to implement, enrich, and support the education program of the school system. This objective will be achieved through the following provisions which apply to all instructional curricula:

- adequate educational materials that reflect a pluralistic society,
- a wide range of materials on all levels of difficulty with diverse appeal and differing points of view,
- a variety of selections that satisfies the personal and recreational reading, listening, and viewing needs of the children enrolled in the school district.

Guidance curricula are chosen by the same specific criteria as all instructional curricula:

1. Are the learning objectives and focus of the program compatible with the school district's educational goals?
2. Are the materials age appropriate for the students involved?
3. Is there support in the research literature for the type of program being evaluated?
4. Is this program based on widely accepted educational techniques?

Appendix B
Sample Curriculum Review Policy

Any adult resident or employee of the school district may raise objection to materials used in the educational program. The staff member receiving the complaint shall report the matter to his/her principal. Every effort should be made to resolve the issue informally at the school or building level. Normally, the material(s) in question will remain in use pending resolution of the objection.

The complainant shall be apprised of the district's selection policy, criteria for selection, and the qualifications of those persons selecting the material. In addition, the complainant will be informed of the reason and purpose for the selection, and the judgement of other outside professionals, such as reviewers, regarding the material. Appropriate district-level personnel should be consulted for their expertise which may contribute to a resolution of the issue.

If the informal, building-level process has been unsuccessful, the complainant may formally challenge the use of specific materials in the educational program. All formal objections to educational materials must be made in writing on the "Request for Reconsideration of Educational Material" form. Each attendance center and the central office will keep on hand sufficient reconsideration request forms. The reconsideration request form must be signed by the complainant and presented to the principal of the school involved in the reconsideration issue. The principal shall forward the formal objection to the appropriate district-level administrator.

Within two weeks of receipt of the formal complaint, the Superintendent of Schools or designee shall file the formal complaint and the material in question with the district's materials review committee for re-evaluation. The task of the materials review committee is to make a recommendation for disposition of the material in question to the district superintendent. Generally, access to challenged materials will not be restricted during the reconsideration or review process. In some circumstances, alternate materials may be requested by parents for their son or daughter.

The materials review committee shall be composed of 11 members:

- one teacher appointed annually by the district superintendent;
- one building-level media specialist designated annually by the district superintendent;

- two members of the school administration (building or central office) appointed annually by the district superintendent;
- five members from the community appointed annually by the PTA Council;
- two high-school students (one from east, one from west) selected annually _____ by a process determined at each high school.

Care should be taken in the appointment process so that the same members are not selected over and over, but some continuity should be provided from year-to-year. The chairperson of the committee shall not be an employee of the school district. The secretary shall be an employee of the district.

The committee shall be constituted each year by October 1, and conduct an initial meeting prior to October 15 at a time and place designated by the district superintendent and made known to members of the committee at least seven days in advance. The annual meeting shall include an election of the chairperson and secretary, a review of past censorship problems and challenges, a review of the selection policy and the specific procedures for handling challenges to the use of educational materials. Special meetings of the review committee are called by the superintendent or designee in the event of formal challenges to educational materials. The review committee should not be expected to meet more than twice monthly nor more than 12 times per year as a general rule. In the event of an overload of challenges, the review committee may appoint a subcommittee of members and/or nonmembers to consolidate challenges and make recommendations to the full committee. The composition of such subcommittees shall approximate the representation on the full committee. The procedure for a meeting dealing with a formal challenge is as follows:

- Copies of the completed and signed reconsideration request form are distributed to review committee members.
- Copies of the challenged material will be distributed to committee members for their review.
- The complainant (if he/she so desires) will be given an opportunity to speak to and expand on the formal challenge.
- Reviews of the material from professional journals and other sources will be distributed to the committee when available.
- The review committee may request that individuals with special knowledge be present to provide information relative to the material in question.

The complainant shall be kept informed by the secretary concerning the status of the complaint and be given notice of all appropriate forthcoming committee meetings. All meetings of the committee are to abide by the provisions of the Wisconsin open-meetings law. The committee's final recommendation will be: (1) to take no removal action, (2) to remove all or part of the challenged material, (3) to allow the use of alternative titles, selected by the appropriate school personnel, or (4) to limit or restrict the educational use of the challenged material. The decision of the review committee is to be based on the appropriateness of the material for its intended educational use.

A decision to sustain a challenge shall not be construed as a judgement against the professional(s) involved in the original selection or use of the material. Requests to reconsider materials which have previously been before the committee must receive approval of a majority of the committee members before the material will again be reconsidered.

The written recommendation of the review committee and its justification shall be forwarded to the Superintendent of Schools for appropriate action, to the complainant, and to the schools in the district from which the complaint originated.

Any review committee recommendation and subsequent decisions by the administration may be appealed to the board of education for a final decision.

Reprinted from *Protecting the Freedom to Learn,* People For the American Way, 1989, with permission.

Note: Since school counseling materials have been in the top ten most frequently challenged materials for the decade 1982-1992, we recommend adding a school counselor to the review committee. Since religious arguments are frequently cited in challenges, we recommend at least one local minister be part of the review committee.

Request for Reconsideration of Education Material

Author _____ Format of Material _____

Title _____

Publisher/Producer _____

Request initiated by _____Telephone _____

Address _____

City _____State _____ Zip Code _____

School in which material is used _____

1. To what in the material do you object? (Please be specific)

_____

2. In your opinion, what harmful effects upon students might
   result from the use of this material? _____ _____

_____

3. Did you review the entire material? Yes _____ No _____

4. Do you preceive any educational value resulting from the
   use of this material? _____

_____

5. Is there any age group of students for which you would
   recommend this material? _____

6. Is there any material on a similar theme that you would
   recommend as a substitute for the material in question?

_____

7. Do you wish to make an oral presentation before the
   review committee? Yes _____ No _____

Date_____Signature _____

Appendix C
Sample Legal Opinion

The legal opinion below was obtained from a law firm representing a school district which was undergoing a challenge to the *"PUMSY"* program. This sample is meant to illustrate some of the key legal points involved in this type of challenge. It is not meant to be used without the advice of legal counsel (PFAW, 1992a, pp. 41-42)..

Re: *PUMSY: In Pursuit of Excellence*

Dear _____

At your request, the undersigned has reviewed the *PUMSY: In Pursuit of Excellence* program. The purpose of such review was to determine if the program in any way violated state or fede ral statues or regulations.

Please be advised that the program does not violate any State or Federal statutes or regulations. There is nothing in the materials or suggested activities which, even remotely, is prohibited to the schools.

Persons opposed to programs such as this, or any programs or activities within the schools frequently refer to the Hatch Act as a basis for such opposition. The Hatch Act, Section 439 (a) of the General Education Provisions Act applies to Federally funded research and experimentation programs and to psychological and psychiatric testing as part of the research projects.

Contrary to the assertions made by some persons, the Hatch Act does not, nor does any statute or regulation, grant parents the authority to prohibit curricula, texts, materials or teaching methods. There is certainly no statute or regulation which permits one group of residents to dictate to the schools what programs may or may not be included in the school's curricula.

The undersigned has read various news articles regarding opposition to this particular program. If the newspaper articles are accurate, some of the comments and statements made are dangerously close to being defamatory to the authors of the program and to staff using the program. Although the First Amendment to the Constitution guarantees freedom of speech, such freedom may not extend to untrue accusations of illegal or immoral conduct.

The undersigned is quite familiar with the programs and policies of the _____ Local School District and the personnel at the _____ Elementary School. There is no question that the district's programs and policies are in accordance with the law and that the school's personnel are acting in the best interests of the students.

Sincerely yours,

Attorney

Greg Brigman and Peggy Moore

Bibliography

American Association for School Administrators. (1993). The far right marches into school governance (Special issue). *The School Administrator, 9*(50).

American School Counselor Association. (1979, 1981). *Organizing for action: Ideas for mobilizing resources on behalf of elementary guidance.* Fall Church, VA: Author.

American School Counselor Association. (1985). *The school counselor and censorship, position statement.* Alexandria, VA: Author.

American School Counselor Association. (1990). *The school counselor and developmental guidance, position statement.* Alexandria, VA: Author.

American School Counselor Association. (1993). Challenges: *The ASCA Counselor, 30* (4). Alexandria, VA: Author.

Aspy, D., & Roebuck, F. (1977). *Kids don't learn from people they don't like.* Amherst, MA: Human Resource Development Press.

Aspy, D., & Roebuck, F. (1982, April). Affective education: Sound investment. *Education Leadership,* 488-493.

Baker, S.C., & Shaw, M.C. (1987). *Improving counseling through primary prevention.* Columbus, OH: Merrill.

Baker, S., Swisher, J., Nadenichek, P., & Popwicz, C. (1984). Measured effects of primary prevention strategies. *The Personnel and Guidance Journal, 62,* 459-464.

Borders, L.D., & Drury, S.M. (1992). Comprehensive school counseling programs: A review for policy makers, and practitioners. *Journal of Counseling and Development, 70,* 487-498.

Braun, C. (1976). Teacher expectation: Sociopsychological dynamics. *Review of Educational Research, 46,* 185-213.

Brookover, W.B. (1969). *Self-concept and achievement.* Paper presented at American Educational Research Association, Los Angeles, CA.

Caine, R., & Caine, G. (1991). *Teaching and the human brain.* Alexandria, VA: Association for Supervision and Curriculum Development.

Carkhuff, R.R. (1982). Affective education in the age of productivity. *Journal of Education Leadership, 39,* 484-487.

Carnegie Council on Adolescent Development. (1989). *Turning points.* New York: Author.

Cartledge, G., & Milburn, J.F. (1978). The case for teaching social skills in the classroom: A review. *Review of Educational Research, 48,* 133-156.

Cobb, H.D., & Richards, H.C. (1983). Efficacy of counseling services in decreasing behavior problems of elementary school children. *Elementary School Guidance and Counseling, 17,* 180-187.

Coopersmith, S. (1981). *Antecedents of self-esteem.* Durham, N.C.: Consulting Psychologists Press.

Deffenbacher, J.L., & Kemper, C.C. (1974). Counseling test anxious sixth graders. *Elementary School Guidance and Counseling, 11,* 277-283.

Donelson, K. (1987). Six statements/questions from the censors. *Phi Delta Kappan, 69*(3); 208-214.

Education Commission of the States (ECS). (1991). *Communicating about restructuring, p.v.-4.* Denver, CO: Author.

Emerson, J. (1993, April 1). CEE makes import on Calif. school district. *Rockford Register Star.*

Farley & Associates Survey Research Corporation. (1989). *National telephone survey of skills for growing parents.* Columbus, OH: Author.

Fege. (1991, March). Censorship in the schools: Parents can protect the freedom to learn. *PTA Today.*

Galbo, J. (1989, October). *The connection between social relationships and academic achievement: A selective review of the literature.* Paper presented at the California Council on Education of Teachers, Irvine, CA.

Galyean, C. (1983). Guided imagery in the curriculum. *Educational Leadership, 40,* 53-58.

Gerler, E.R. (1980). A longitudinal study of multimodal approaches to small group psychological education. *The School Counselor, 27,* 184-190.

Gerler, E.R. (1985). Elementary school counseling research and the classroom learning environment. *Elementary School Guidance and Counseling, 20*(1), 39-48.

Gerler, E.R., & Anderson, R.F. (1986). The effects of classroom guidance on children's success in school. *Journal of Counseling and Development, 65,* 78-81.

Gerler, E.R. (1992). What we know about school counseling: A reaction to Borders and Drury. *Journal of Counseling and Development, 70,* 499-510.

Gerler, E.R., Kinney, J., & Anderson, R.F. (1985). The effects of counseling on classroom performance. *Journal of Humanistic Education and Development, 23,* 155-165.

Gerstein & Lichtman. (1990). *The best for our kids: Exemplary elementary guidance and counseling programs.* Alexandria, VA: American School Counselor Association.

Glasser, W. (1969). *Schools without failure.* New York: Harper and Row.

Glosoff, H.L., & Koprowicz, C.L. (1990). *Children achieving potential.* Alexandria, VA: American Association for Counseling and Development and the National Conference of State Legislatures.

Gurney, P. (1987). Self-esteem enhancement in children: A review of research findings. *Educational Research, 29*(2), 130-136.

Gysbers, N. (1990). *Building comprehensive school counseling programs.* Greensboro, NC: ERIC/CAPS.

Hadley, H. (1988). Improving reading scores through a self-esteem intervention program. *Elementary School Guidance and Counseling, 22*(3), 248-252.

Halgren, E., Wilson, C.L., Squires, N.K., Engel, J., Walter, R.D., & Crandal, P. H. (1983). Dynamics of the Hippocampal contribution to memory. In W. Seifert, *Molecular, cellular, and behavioral neurobiology of the Hippocampus.* New York: Academic Press.

Hill, B.M. (1983). *Effective child guidance: An educator's guidebook.* Ft. Lauderdale, FL: Nova University. (ERIC Document Reproduction Service No. ED 258 702)

Hoffman, L.R. (1991). Developmental counseling for prekindergarten children: A preventive approach. *Elementary School Guidance and Counseling, 26,* 56-66.

Hohenshil, T., & Brown, M. (1991). Public school counseling services for prekindergarten children. *Elementary School Guidance and Counseling, 2,* 4-11.

Hoge, R.D., & Luce, S. (1979). Predicting academic achievement from classroom behavior. *Review of Educational research, 49,* 479-496.

Jones, J.L. (1990). *What's left after the right?* Federal Way, WA: Washington Education Association.

Jones, J.L. (1993). Targets of the right. *American School Board Journal, 180*(4), 22-29.

Kaplan, L., & Geoffroy, K. (1987). The Hatch Amendment: A primer for counselors, part II. *The School Counselor, 35,* 88-95.

Katz, L.G. (1986). *Implications of recent research for kindergarten curriculum.* (ERIC Document Reproduction service No. ED 274 463)

Lakoff, G. (1987). *Women, fire, and dangerous things.* Chicago: University of Chicago Press.

Marsh, H.W. (1984). Relations among dimensions of self-attributing dimensions of self-concept and academic achievements. *Journal of Educational Psychology, 76*(6), 1291-1308.

Matthews, D. (1989). Relaxation theory for rural youth. *Research Bulletin No. 48.* Washington, DC: Cooperative State Research Services, United States Department of Agriculture.

McCarthy, M.M. (1993). Challenges to the public school curriculum: New targets and strategies. *Phi Delta Kappan, 75*(1), 55-60.

McGuiness, D., & Pribram, K. (1980). The neuropsychology of attention. In M.D. Wittrock, *The brain and psychology.* New York: Academic Press.

Morris, C. (1992) Pressure groups and the politics of education: Updating school board policies. *National Education Policy Network of the National School Boards Association, 23*(9), 1-5.

Mullis, I., Dossey, J., Jones, L., & Gentile, C. (1991). *Trends in academic progress: Achievement of U.S. students in science 1969-1990, mathematics 1973-1990, reading 1971-1990, and writing 1984-1990.* Princeton, NJ: Educational Testing Service.

Myrick, R.D. (1993). *Developmental guidance and counseling: A practical approach,* (2nd ed.). Minneapolis, MN: Educational Media corporation.

Nagel-Harmon, D. (1989). *Measurement of effects on self-esteem following participation in PUMSY In pursuit of excellence program.* Unpublished dissertation, Central Missouri State University.

National Association for the Education of Young Children. (1986). Position statement on developmentally appropriate practice in early childhood programs serving children from birth through age 8, 4-19.

National Association of Elementary School Principals. (1990). *Early childhood education: Standards for quality programs for young children.* Alexandria, VA: Author.

National Education Association. (undated). Far right attacks on the NEA, Why?, An Information/Awareness/Training Packet for Members, Washington, DC: Author.

The National PTA. *The national PTA's guide to extremism* Chicago, IL: Author.

Orstein, R., & Sobel, D. (1987). *The healing brain: Breakthrough discoveries about how the brain keeps us healthy.* New York: Simon and Schuster.

People For the American Way. (1991). *Attacks on the freedom to learn, 1990-1991 annual report.* Washington, DC: Author.

People For the American Way. (1992a). *Attacks on the freedom to learn, 1991-92 report.* Washington, DC: Author.

People For the American Way. (1992b). *The new target: Far right attacks on self-esteem programs.* Washington, DC: Author.

People For the American Way. (1989). *Protecting the freedom to learn, A citizen's guide.* Washington, DC: Author.

Peterson, M., & Poppen, W. (1992a). *Challenges to and censorship of school guidance materials.* Greensboro, NC: ERIC, EDOCG9210.

Peterson, M., & Poppen, W. (1992b). *School counselors and the first freedom.* Paper presented at the 1992 annual convention of the American Association for Counseling and Development, Baltimore, MD.

Purkey, W.W. (1970). *Self-concept and school achievement.* Englewood Cliffs, NJ: Prentice Hall.

Quest International. (1991a). *Highlights of skills for growing student testing.* Granville, OH: Author.

Quest International. (1991b). *Profile of Lions-Quest principals.* Granville, OH: Author.

Reithman, H. (1990). Censorship and selection: Issues and answers for schools. *American Library.* American Association of School Administrators.

Sanders, M.C. (1991). *Responses to typical concerns of challengers: Report to the board of eduation on PUMSY in pursuit of excellence.* Westchester, IL: Westchester Public School District 92.5.

United States Department of Education. (1987). *Eight pointers on teaching children to think. Research in brief.* IS87-104Rib. Washington, DC: Author.

United States Department of Labor Secretary's Commission on Achieving Necessary Skills. (1991). *What work requires of schools: A SCANS report for America 2000.* Washington, DC: Author.

Wehlage, G.G., & Rutter, R. A. (1986). Dropping out: How much do schools contribute to the problem? *Teachers College Record, 87*(3), 374-392.

Wirth, S. (1977). Effect of a multifaceted reading program on self-concept. *Elementary School Guidance and Counseling, 12,* 33-40.

Wooster, A.D., & Carson, A. (1982). Improved reading and self-concept through communication and social skills training. *British Journal of Guidance and Counseling, 10,* 83-87.

Greg Brigman and Peggy Moore